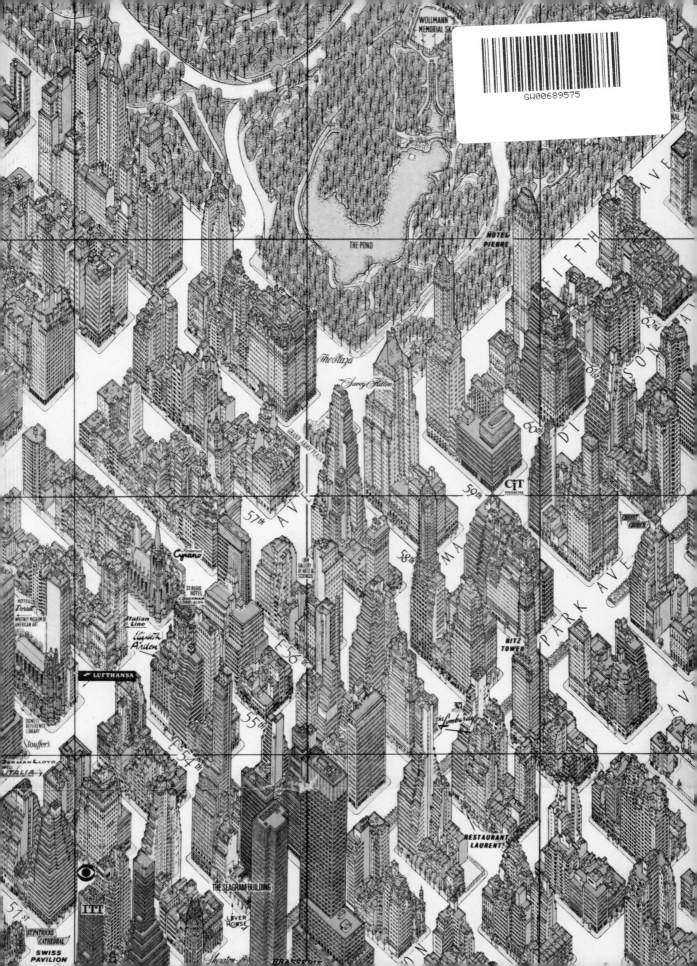

THE CITY

YESTERDAY, TODAY AND TOMORROW

THE CITY

YESTERDAY, TODAY AND TOMORROW

EMRYS JONES and
ELEANOR VAN ZANDT

Aldus Books · Jupiter Books

Designer   Susan Cook
Research   Naomi Narod
           Lynette Trotter
           Ann Mitchell

First published in 1974 by
Aldus Books Limited, Aldus House,
17 Conway Street, London W1P 6BS
and Jupiter Books, 167 Hermitage Road,
Harringay, London N4 1LZ

SBN 490 00261 7

Printed and bound in Spain by
Novograph S.L. and Roner S.A.
Crta. de Irun Km. 12,450
Madrid 34
Dep. Legal : M. 17.705-1974.

Contents

The Cross, The Circle, and Beyond

1

Nearly 2,000 years of city life have elapsed since the Romans founded Londinium here beside the Thames. This view of modern London—with its mixture of government buildings, merchant vessels, offices, churches, and construction cranes—suggests some of the varied functions of a great city. At left in the picture: The *Discovery*, a sailing ship now visited as a museum. In the background, the majestic dome of St. Paul's Cathedral.

THE WORLD WE LIVE IN is becoming more and more urban. Today, most Americans and Europeans live in or near a city. In the United States and Canada, more than 70 per cent of the people live in urban areas having a population of 100,000 or more. In Britain, the urban population is 80 per cent: that is, four out of every five Britons live in towns. In many other industrialized nations the urban population makes up well over half the total: in Belgium, for example, it is 63 per cent, in Japan 64 per cent, in West Germany 77 per cent.

Of course, many parts of the world are still mainly rural. But the developing countries, also, are experiencing the trend toward urbanization. In 1920, 13 million people in Latin America (14 per cent of the total population) lived in towns of over 20,000, but by 1960 this figure had already risen to 68 million (32 per cent). All over Latin America, country people are flocking to the cities in great numbers in search of jobs. By contrast, only a very small percentage of Africans and Asians live in cities—although some Asian cities, such as Calcutta, are huge and densely populated.

One dramatic aspect of today's urban scene is the growth of the very big cities. In 1900, there were 11 cities in the world having populations of more than 1 million. Today, there are 130 of these "million" cities. Some of them have grown to an enormous size. Greater London, for example, takes in an area of 620 square miles and has a population of nearly $7\frac{1}{2}$ million. Its entire metropolitan area (including towns whose inhabitants work mainly in London) has a population of more than $11\frac{1}{2}$ million. New

York is equally large. Its metropolitan area houses 11,529,000 people. Tokyo has grown even more enormous. The population of its conurbation, which includes the city of Yokohama, grew from 9,049,000 in 1950 to 13,746,000 by 1970—an increase of more than 50 per cent within the space of 20 years.

In the face of such phenomenal growth, municipal and national governments are increasingly devoting large amounts of time, money, and thought to the future of our cities. Concerned citizens, also, are beginning to realize that the process of urbanization contains the possibility of choosing between alternatives, and that even the individual can help to influence the choice, and so share in city planning.

One area of concern is the pattern of urban growth. The physical expansion of the city inevitably involves some destruction of the countryside. In many western countries, growth in the form of "suburban sprawl" continues to devour great chunks of land, making open countryside less and less accessible to city dwellers. In small, densely populated countries, such as the Netherlands and Britain, containing this sprawl is a major challenge. Various plans have been adopted in these countries to keep development within boundaries and so to preserve the precious green space. In the United States, the abundance of land has tended to encourage its lavish exploitation. But even so, certain parts of the U.S.A. are running out of open space. Urban sprawl along the northeast coast, between Washington and Boston, is turning that part of the country into one huge megalopolis ("BosWash"). Such formless growth dismays people who love both city and country and feel that we need to maintain some balance and distinction between the two.

The quality of life within the city itself is another area of concern. Cities have always had environmental problems of one kind or another. Two hundred years ago, a city dweller could expect unpaved, muddy streets and polluted water. Today, city streets are paved and water is purified, but new problems, such as air pollution and traffic congestion, have taken the place of the old problems.

In spite of various ills, most cities are exciting places. Every year, people travel thousands of miles to see the world's great cities. They visit the glittering giants—London, Rome, New York, Rio de Janeiro—but they also visit smaller cities that have some special charm, such as Salzburg, Isfahan, and Quebec. A few cities have an almost legendary appeal. "Good Americans, when they die," observed a 19th-century wit, "go to Paris." Generations of travelers from all over the world have found Paris elegant, historic, lively, romantic, and captivating. Venice, perhaps even more than Paris, has also captured the romantic imagination. Its canals and gondolas, pink and white palaces and gilded churches, now gradually sinking into the Adriatic Sea, make it the dream city of the world.

Other cities have attractions of a different kind. Belching smokestacks and a converging network of highways and railroad tracks are, as much as busloads of tourists, indications of a city's magnetic power.

Today, our idea of the city is changing. There is a basic difference between a city

Perhaps more than any other city, Paris seems to have
been designed to delight the eye. Splendid monuments,
grand boulevards, and spacious parks (above, the
Tuileries Gardens looking toward the Place de la
Concorde and the Arc de Triomphe) express the French
love of order and elegance. Below: San Francisco's
Fisherman's Wharf—a colorful section of one of
America's liveliest and most cosmopolitan cities.

Below: 20 minutes from Piccadilly Circus—a place to "get away from it all" without leaving London. The green slopes of Hampstead Heath are perfect for walking the dog, flying a kite, or just listening to the birds and the distant hum of traffic.

such as Portland, Oregon, which covers 80 square miles and has 375,000 people, and a megalopolis such as "BosWash," which sprawls along 500 miles of Atlantic coastline. Modern methods of communication and transport are making it possible for people to live an essentially "urban" life and yet live miles away from anything that we should recognize as a city center. Twenty years from now when we speak of a city, we might mean something as sprawling as "BosWash," or something as compact as a single, giant skyscraper, containing shops, offices, and living space for several thousand people.

Traditional cities—however much they vary from one country to another—have certain features in common. One of these features is density.

Whether a community is relatively small and classified as a "town" or relatively large and classified as a "city," its people live close together. Density was characteristic of ancient cities (the Psalmist observed, "Jerusalem is built as a city that is compact together") and it is characteristic of most modern cities as well.

The earliest known symbol for a city is an ancient Egyptian hieroglyph: a cross within a circle. The cross represents a central point where people, power, and resources are concentrated. The circle suggests an enclosure, or boundary. For many centuries this boundary took the form of a wall, which gave the city protection. In time of war, the city gates would be shut and soldiers stationed on top of the wall to repel attackers.

Modern warfare has rendered the wall useless, and town walls today have only a picturesque value. But the ideal of the circle—of a boundary of some sort—persists. Politically, the circle is the "city limits." There is a line around the city, beyond which the city government has no jurisdiction.

Visually, the circle is harder to recognize. In the case of small cities, the built-up area may end roughly at the city limits. Some cities—notably London—are surrounded

11

by "greenbelts," areas maintained as open countryside to check the spread of the city. But in the case of many other large cities, the circle has virtually disappeared. A city such as Chicago or Manchester doesn't stop; it just fades away.

But although the circle may be fading, the cross remains a distinctive and essential characteristic of all cities, even though it has many forms and many meanings. In its simplest form, the cross might be the intersection of Main and Broad Streets in Anytown, U.S.A., location of Smith's Department Store, the Downtown Bank, the Central Hotel, and the County Courthouse. It is the central point for the town itself, and for the surrounding area.

More often, the cross is not a literal crossroads, but a square, a single important

The cross and the circle appear in the towns and villages of many different cultures throughout the world. Below: A Mexican fishing village built in a lagoon on the Pacific coast, a striking example of the cross and circle.

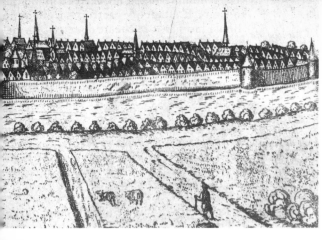

In the past, many cities built walls for protection against attack. The city of Tienen, in Belgium, shown left as it appeared in the 1600s, was protected by a wall and a river as well. Below: The city of Carcassonne, in southern France, one of the best-preserved of medieval walled cities.

street, or a whole neighborhood. In Vienna, it is the whole length of the Kärntnerstrasse, with the Opera at one end, St. Stephen's Cathedral at the other, and elegant shops in between. In Moscow, it is the Kremlin and neighboring Red Square—once a year the scene of the May Day parade, and every day the scene of long lines of people filing past Lenin's tomb. New York's Wall Street area is the financial "crossroads" for the United States, and to some extent for the western world as a whole. In the old city of Jerusalem, the temple area has become, over the course of centuries, a spiritual "crossroads" for three major religions: Judaism, Christianity, and Islam.

These few examples illustrate the point that the cross represents various aspects of a city's and a nation's life. A town or city is, first of all, a crossroads in a political sense. It is the seat of a government that has authority perhaps over a surrounding country area, perhaps over a province, perhaps over a whole nation. It may be a religious crossroads as well. (In England, incidentally, most cathedral towns are called "cities", even if they are quite small—the city of Ely, for example, has only about 10,000 people.) And a city is always an economic crossroads —a place for buying and selling, and often for producing manufactured goods.

Within a city, there are often several meeting-points for each function. So a more accurate symbol for the city today would be a circle with several crosses, instead of one. In London, for example, there are several major shopping districts, which cater for people living and working in different parts of this very large city. Even a much less

13

complex city, such as Ibadan in Nigeria, may have many separate markets, open at different times. At Ibadan's night markets one can buy cooked food, which many people then eat at the market. These night markets have thus become social "crossroads" as well as commercial ones.

The mingling of activities in one place has been typical of cities from early times. Cathedral and marketplace, inn and theater, waterfront and shops, are only a few of the combinations that appear in the life of cities. In Islamic cities one can see a striking example of a multipurpose area in the mosques, whose courtyards are filled not only with worshipers but also with students learning their lessons, women gossiping, and old men just sitting around.

The mixture of activities reflects the interdependence that exists among different groups within the city. One function attracts another. In the Middle Ages, London was just a small area (now called "the City") including the Tower of London, old St. Paul's Cathedral, and the north bank of the Thames. It was a center of trade. Here lived the merchants who controlled the trade; the craftsmen who fashioned imported raw materials into finished articles, such as gloves and armor; and the shopkeepers who sold the products. Merchants lived above their businesses and as near as possible to the other merchants with whom they dealt every day. The exchanges were established in the same neighborhood and within easy reach of the bankers who loaned money to the merchants. "Intelligence"—that is, news of cargoes and shipping movements, of wars and pestilence—was communicated in the area around St. Paul's Cathedral (probably because it was a natural meeting place).

Below: Women selling vegetables in a street market in Peru. At right: A market scene in Maiduguri, in Nigeria. Markets of one kind or another play an important part in the life of all towns and cities.

The splendor of the Piazza San Marco in Venice (left) more than compensates for its plague of pigeons. On summer evenings an orchestra plays in the square, and the floodlit façade of the cathedral gives the scene an aura of timeless mystery. Below: Café-sitting remains a popular pastime in Paris. A table at the Deux Magots offers one a fine view of the passing scene along the Boulevard St.-Germain.

15

Right: Milan's Galleria
Vittorio Emanuele is the
most spectacular of the
traditional Italian covered
streets. Here, one can
shop, have an *espresso*,
meet a friend, or simply
stroll, away from wheeled
traffic and protected
from hot sun or showers.

When "intelligence" became organized into
more regular "news" and began to be
printed, it remained centered in this
neighborhood. Today, this area, especially
Fleet Street, is still the center of British
journalism.

Until cities became mechanized, face-to-
face contact was the main way of doing
business. Messages could be sent, of course,
but a conversation, then as now, was often
preferable. With no telephone and slow
transport, people had to work within easy
distance of one another, especially if their
businesses were related.

Today's advanced systems of communication and transport have certainly lessened the
need for such centralization. A company's
factory can be located hundreds of miles
away from its head office—perhaps in a very
small town. Long-distance telephone service
and air travel make this possible. In theory,
head offices, too, could be located outside the
big cities. But most executives continue to
prefer the metropolis. Their work often
requires them to make quick decisions in
conjunction with other people, and for this
there is no satisfactory substitute for face-to-
face contact.

Certain industries find it necessary to be
located in particular cities. For example,
most big American advertising agencies need
to be near the communications media—
especially television and magazines—which
means locating in New York City. The U.S.
garment industry, also centered mainly in
New York, receives twice a year an influx of
buyers from all over the country, who go
from one manufacturer to another to inspect
the new models and place their orders. If

Industry and trade are
the lifeblood of a city.
Some cities attract the
whole of a particular
industry: New York's
garment district supplies
the entire United States
with ready-to-wear clothes.
The mass media and book
publishing are other New
York-based industries.

Entertainment of all kinds—from lively, open-air band concerts, such as this one in St. James's Park, London, to the most sophisticated and intellectual drama— enrich the lives of city dwellers. The big cities have the resources of talent and the large audiences to support a varied cultural life throughout the year. At right: Tokyo's Nichigeki Theater, where one can attend performances of plays and musicals.

this industry were scattered here and there throughout the United States, the retail stores would have a much more expensive and time-consuming task in selecting their stock, and manufacturers located in out-of-the-way places would soon go out of business.

The arts also tend to concentrate in a few great cities, which seem to act as catalysts in the creative process. For a young artist, the big city offers the best in training, the stimulation of other talents and new ideas, and an

The interchange of ideas helps to make a city a stimulating place in which to live. Most of the world's cities have at least one college or university, which helps to enrich its cultural and political life. At left, some students at an American university.

atmosphere of excitement—of things happening, or about to happen.

This intangible quality of "things happening," which all cities possess in varying degrees, attracts all sorts of people—not only artists and executives. A Greek philosopher observed that it is not houses and walls that make a city, "but men able to use their opportunities." In spite of the vexing problems they face—pollution, crime, and the rest—certain cities continue to attract people from all over the world seeking these opportunities. The number of young Australians, for example, who come to London (an estimated 100,000 a year), making a journey of 13,500 miles, at very considerable cost, to live in a tiny "bedsitter" or share an apartment with three or four other people,

suggests that the opportunities are not entirely economic ones. Jobs are plentiful in Australia's thriving cities. But London, and a few other cities, are "special." They are meeting places, not only for goods and services, but often for ideas and for different cultures and ways of life. The cities that have realized their potential as cultural crossroads are the ones that exert the strongest attraction. With cities, as with individuals, "nothing succeeds like success."

But urban civilizations do eventually decline for various reasons, and others rise to take their place. In the chapters that follow, we shall look at some of these civilizations and at the changing face of the city throughout the world, from ancient times to the present. Finally, we shall

Is this the shape of cities to come? The Hexahedron, designed by architect and philosopher Paolo Soleri, is one of many revolutionary designs for tomorrow's urban living. The structure would be 3,609 feet high with a total covered surface of 140 acres, intended to accommodate a population of 170,000—an average density of 1,214 people per acre. Soleri has coined the word "arcology," from "architecture" and "ecology," to denote his complex and compact urban structures, of which Hexahedron is only one. To be truly efficient and provide a more supportive environment for humans, a city, Soleri believes, must contract—facilitating human interaction and eliminating the wastefulness and pollution of present cities. Hexahedron would have no automobiles; people would get about by elevators and escalators, and by walking.

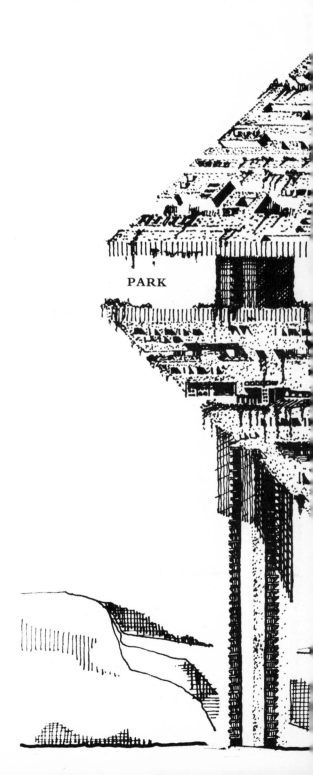

PARK

speculate a bit about the cities of tomorrow.

Plenty of possibilities lie ahead for the city. There is the possibility of formless, unplanned growth. There is the possibility of deliberately dispersing the city—of breaking up the high density of the big centers and creating instead a scattered kind of city similar to the open suburban landscapes we already know. There is the possibility, preferred by many city planners, of doing the opposite: of re-concentrating the suburban sprawl into various kinds of high-density units. Imaginative schemes for transforming the urban environment are coming off drawing boards while you read this book. They envisage cities consisting of one enormous building, cities built under the earth, cities floating on the sea, cities shaped like giant wheels, cities covered with plastic domes as protection from the elements.

The possibilities exist. Choosing among them is one of the major challenges of our time. The individual citizen may have little choice in the overall planning of his city. But he can, as a voter, bring some influence to bear on specific matters—for example, on the relative appropriations given to public transport and to highway construction, and on the zoning of areas to include or exclude apartment houses, business, and industry.

The first step is to decide what we want in a city. In doing so, we shall find it useful to know something about many kinds of cities in many parts of the world. As we learn about them, we may discover certain features that we want to adapt in our own cities. We may also gain a clearer idea of what a city can be—an exciting place, sometimes a beautiful place, and occasionally the scene of man's greatest achievements.

20

Ancient Cities

2

Some of the grandeur of Thebes, capital of Egypt for hundreds of years, has survived in the columns of the Temple of Amon, at nearby Karnak. Even more than in other ancient civilizations, religion was the keystone of Egyptian cities. The tombs and temples have long outlasted the palaces of the pharaohs—not to mention the shops and the houses of ordinary people.

THE FIRST CITY-DWELLERS lived in the Middle East, more than 5,000 years ago. Some lived in Egypt, some in part of what is now Iraq—the ancient land called Mesopotamia—some in Palestine. Recent evidence suggests that the first city ever built may have been Jericho, of biblical fame. This part of the world—the Mediterranean lands and western Asia—is often called "the Cradle of Civilization," because it produced a series of cultures that are considered the direct "ancestors" of modern Western civilization.

But other parts of the world have their own urban traditions. The people of the Indus Valley in what is now Pakistan were building cities 4,000 years ago. Northern China also began developing its own forms of urban life in prehistoric times. And when—several millennia later—the Spanish Conquistadors arrived in the New World, they found splendid cities built by the Aztec, Maya, and Inca Indians.

The early cities of the Americas and those of the ancient world were largely destroyed by their conquerors. Those cities that have escaped invasion have suffered the more gradually destructive forces of time and weather. What the first cities looked like, how they developed, and what sort of life they offered their inhabitants are puzzles that are still being pieced together by archaeologists.

One conclusion the archaeologists have reached is that the city grew out of the village. Even the village appeared only after hundreds of thousands of years of man's existence on earth. In earliest times men lived by hunting and collecting food, picking such plants as grew wild, and moving around when necessary to take advantage of a better food supply. Then, some time between 9000 B.C. and 5000 B.C. in the Middle East, men learned how to cultivate plants and domesticate animals.

As they learned how to cultivate the land, people began to live in settled communities. Cultivation greatly increased the productivity of the land, and the greater abundance of food must have caused an unprecedented growth in population. Many existing villages grew larger, and new ones appeared and expanded. Gradually, the larger settlements acquired some imposing features: a shrine or a temple, a citadel or fortress, an encircling wall.

Underlying this change in appearance was another change in economics. In the village, each farmer had produced enough food to sustain himself and his family. Each villager was also his own craftsman, making the implements he needed to plow the fields and harvest his crops, fashioning the pots in which to cook his food, weaving the cloth to make his own garments. The village may have produced enough extra food to support a religious leader of some kind and perhaps to pay for the services of an itinerant crafts-

man who served several communities. But aside from this, the members of the community were self-sufficient, though on a rather primitive level.

It was only when the community began to produce a surplus of food that the city became possible. In the Middle East—even in the relatively fertile valleys of the Nile, Tigris, and Euphrates—increasing the productivity of the land required irrigation. And irrigation required considerable organization of labor. Some form of government had to evolve in order to direct this communal effort, and in most cases the government took the form of a monarchy. The early kings probably obtained power by the usual means—personal strength, bravery,

Where planes now land at London's Heathrow Airport, some ancient Britons once lived in a village that may have resembled the one in this drawing (right), based on archaeological evidence dated between 500 and 300 B.C. The building in the foreground is a temple. Below: This village in the Sudan gives some idea of pre-urban communities.

talent for organization, cunning—and many maintained this power partly through identification with religion. A king might also be the high priest, or even be venerated as a god himself, in human form. Thus he could command absolute allegiance from the people. He could induce them to do virtually anything, from growing more food to fighting battles and building cities.

The extra food that the farmers produced was used to support other members of the community. Freed from their dependence on the land, these people could pursue other occupations and provide services in exchange for the food they received. Society split into economic classes: artisans of various kinds, merchants, priests, and war-

riors. Gradually, complex urban societies grew out of simple peasant communities.

Having control of the surplus, the king and priests were free to allocate part of this capital to ambitious building programs. They built granaries in which to store the surplus; citadels and walls to protect the population in case of an enemy attack; and palaces, pyramids, and temples that expressed their ideas about the universe and man's place in it. All these monumental structures reflected the growing power and wealth of the city.

Exempted from manual labor, the priestly class could devote their time to mental activity. Their responsibility for administering the surplus and directing the life of the

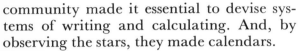
The ziggurat of Ur, made of bricks, has been remarkably well preserved by centuries of burial in debris. Its basic shape (above) is still intact, even though the corners have been worn down. A reconstruction (above, left) shows how it may have looked originally.

community made it essential to devise systems of writing and calculating. And, by observing the stars, they made calendars.

The invention of writing is generally regarded as the beginning of civilization. It certainly marked the beginning of the long association between urban life and creative thought. Although some great ideas and works of art have been conceived in rural surroundings, the city has always been the main incubator of genius. Its ruling classes have provided a market for the work of artists and scholars. And its stimulating atmosphere has attracted original thinkers of every kind, who in turn attract others. This aspect of the city is apparent in the Latin word for city, *civitas*, to which our word "civilization" is related. As we trace the development of some ancient cities, we can see that their stories are also the story of the growth of civilized man.

An urban evolution such as we have described must have taken place in the foothills of the Zagros Mountains of Mesopotamia some 5,000 years ago. Over the course of centuries, people moved from their mountain settlements down into the valleys of the Tigris and Euphrates rivers. In this land, called Sumer, they built several great cities.

One of them, the city of Ur, stood on the banks of the Euphrates near the place where, 4,000 years ago, the river flowed into the

Persian Gulf. (Today, silt deposits have moved the coastline south.) Ur was surrounded by a wall. Within the wall, which was roughly oval in shape and 26 feet high, the buildings pressed closely together. They were built of sun-baked brick. Most of the dwellings uncovered by archaeologists were two stories high and some had as many as seven rooms. They were built around courtyards, as houses in Iraq still are today.

The pattern of building in Ur seems to have been largely determined by the owners of individual plots of land. This accounts for the tortuous streets and the occasional jutting-out of a house into the street. Selfish building practices were sometimes discouraged by admonitions such as this: "If a house blocks the main street in its building, the owner of the house will die; if a house overhangs or obstructs the side of the main street, the heart of the dweller in that house will not be glad."

Most of the estimated 25,000 people who lived within the city walls worked the fields outside them. This system contrasts sharply with the modern western city, whose food surplus is supplied from farmers living on the land, but it does have a modern parallel in some of the cities of West Africa, in which

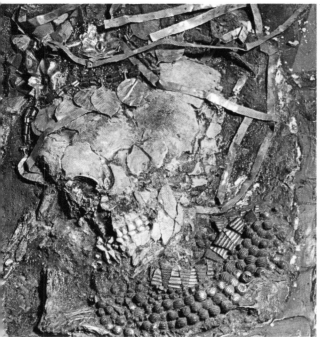

most of the city-dwellers are also farmers.

By examining Sumerian inscriptions on clay tablets and the imprints left by seeds in moist clay pots, archaeologists have discovered what crops the people planted and what animals they raised. Barley was the main crop, and some of it was used to brew beer. A payroll found in the temple at Erech, another Sumerian city, includes a series of what are probably personal names, each followed by words meaning "beer and bread for one day." Wheat was also grown, and dates, grapes, and apples. Fish was the main source of protein. Sheep and goats were raised mainly for milk and wool. Within the temple precincts these products were processed, stored, and distributed to the community.

The sacred enclosure, or *temenos*, dominated the city of Ur. Located near the center of the city, it included within its walls the Temple of the Moon God and a great stepped pyramid, or ziggurat, part of which is still standing. Long stairways on ramps led to the top of the ziggurat, where there was a small temple, assumed to be a haven for the gods. The Mesopotamian ziggurats appear to have represented mountains, which were believed to be dwelling places

27

Early Civilizations Throughout the World

These maps show the locations of the early civilizations described in this chapter. The rectangular areas marked on the map of the world, at right, correspond to the five other maps.

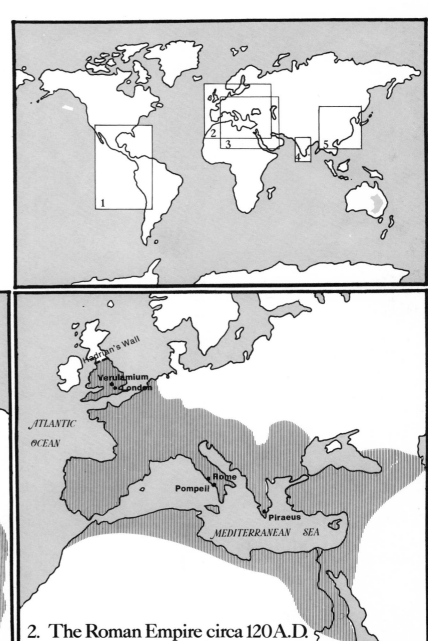

1. **Civilizations of the New World**

2. **The Roman Empire circa 120 A.D.**

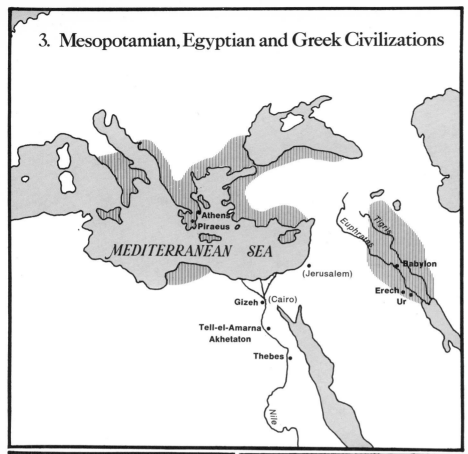

3. Mesopotamian, Egyptian and Greek Civilizations

Athens
Piraeus
MEDITERRANEAN SEA
Euphrates
Tigris
Babylon
(Jerusalem)
Erech
Ur
Gizeh (Cairo)
Tell-el-Amarna
Akhetaton
Thebes
Nile

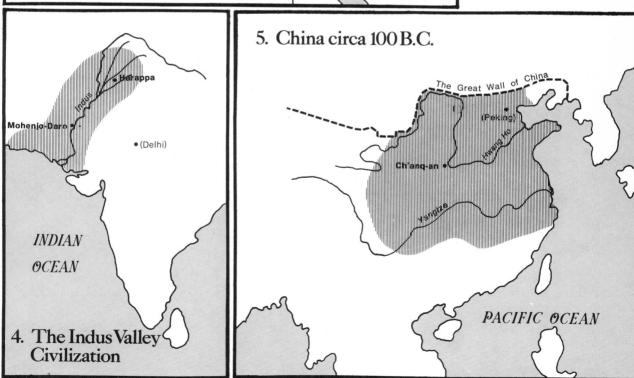

4. The Indus Valley Civilization

Harappa
Indus
Mohenjo-Daro
(Delhi)
INDIAN
OCEAN

5. China circa 100 B.C.

The Great Wall of China
(Peking)
Ch'ang-an
Hwang Ho
Yangtze
PACIFIC OCEAN

of the gods and which were, in fact, the birthplace of Sumerian culture. Unlike the pyramids of Egypt, they were not tombs.

But Ur did have its royal tombs. These were discovered by archaeologists just outside the sacred enclosure. They yielded a dazzling collection of jewelry and other gold objects. Many of these adorned the skeletons of the king and queen and of the courtiers who accompanied the bodies of their sovereigns into the grave.

Farther north on the Euphrates, a later Mesopotamian people, the Babylonians, built one of the world's most splendid cities. During Babylon's long and tempestuous history—spanning more than 1,000 years—it was destroyed by the Assyrians, rebuilt, and destroyed again. Once more it was rebuilt in the seventh century B.C., under King Nebuchadnezzar, who conquered the Jews and took them as slaves to his city. This, the Babylon of the Old Testament, was a vast city of some 300,000 to 400,000 people. It was the center of an empire that extended as far as Egypt, and the wealth of that empire was reflected in the city's magnificence. The very word "Babylonian" has come to mean "luxurious" or "splendid."

According to legend, it was Nebuchadnezzar who built for his queen the famous "hanging gardens," a series of terraces planted with a profusion of flowers, shrubs, and trees. Another landmark of the city was the biblical "Tower of Babel," a massive ziggurat nearly 300 feet high.

In the fourth century B.C., Babylon was taken by Alexander the Great. It became a capital and a meeting point for east and west. But its decline was imminent. The builders of later cities used Babylon as a vast quarry, leaving only its name and legends of its former glory.

Compared to Mesopotamia, Egypt offers surprisingly little evidence of its ancient urban culture. Many structures remain, but they are nearly all tombs and temples. Houses and streets are almost nonexistent. Most Egyptians lived on farms, and only a

The legendary magnificence of Babylon is conveyed by this impression of *The Construction of the Tower of Babel* by the painter Hendrick van Cleve. According to the Bible the tower was built at a time when all people belonged to one race. To punish them for their arrogance in trying to build a tower that would reach up to Heaven, God made them speak different languages so that they could not understand each other and had to abandon the project.

minority in the provincial market towns that seem to have been the main form of urban settlement.

The pharaoh and his court lived in the capital city. But until the establishment of Thebes as the capital in about 2000 B.C., each pharaoh built his own capital near the site where his tomb was under construction. This shows the relative importance of tomb and capital city for the Egyptians.

The Egyptians reserved their building skill—and their rich stone deposits—for the dead, rather than for the living. The pyramids they built are the largest and most impressive tombs the world has ever seen. Long after Egypt's ancient cities have crumbled and disappeared, the pyramids still stand, monuments to the Egyptian belief in the divinity of their kings and an afterlife that was much longer and more important than their stay on earth. Apart from some magnificent temples, the pyramids are the true monuments of Egyptian civilization.

The largest of these tombs is the Great Pyramid, or the Pyramid of Cheops. This pyramid contains some 2,300,000 blocks of stone, each weighing an average of $2\frac{1}{2}$ tons. Its construction took 30 years and the labor of 100,000 men. Its base—a near-perfect square—covers an area slightly over 13 acres, more than the combined areas of the United States Capitol and the British Houses of Parliament. The orientation of

the sides is almost exactly north-south, east-west. The angles are only a hairbreadth from being right angles.

All this indicates a very sophisticated society, able to use its resources with great skill. It also shows that the Egyptians had already developed considerable skill in computation, astronomy, and building.

The thousands of workers employed in building a pyramid lived near the site. Some idea of their living conditions can be inferred from a site near the modern town of Tell-el-Amarna. Ruins of a workers' walled village consist of a number of straight parallel streets with nearly identical row houses, and there are no spaces for gardens. Adjacent to the workers' village at Tell-el-Amarna are the ruins of the capital itself, the city of Akhetaton. This city was built in about 1375 B.C. by the Pharaoh Ikhnaton, who, having converted to the worship of the sun-god, wanted a new capital, away from Thebes and the priests of the god Amon. The new capital was a spacious city whose airy, open buildings and terraced gardens harmonized with the new official religion of sun-worship.

Some of the houses were still under construction when Ikhnaton died. The "new regime" moved the capital back to Thebes, and Akhetaton was abandoned. It had been a living city for just over 15 years.

Thebes, the capital of Egypt for many centuries, was at the peak of its glory in the 14th century B.C. From conquered lands, the pharaohs brought back riches to embellish their city. Of this city, hardly a trace remains. But nearby Karnak's great temples and tombs survived attacks by the Assyrians and later conquerors.

The Greek poet Homer describes Thebes as the "hundred-gated"—referring, probably, to the gates of the many temple enclosures. Today, even after being used on occasions as stone quarries, these monumental buildings are spectacular evidence of the wealth of ancient Egypt.

Running southward to the sea, through what is now Pakistan, is the Indus River. In the valley of this river, more than 4,000 years ago, another civilization flourished. Its two largest cities, Harappā and Mohenjo-daro, are among several that have been excavated by archaeologists.

Each of these cities was dominated by a citadel, a mound of earth on which were located various public buildings as well as a protecting wall. The citadel at Harappā has only foundations to show. At Mohenjo-daro, 400 miles south, extensive ruins have revealed much about this Asian civilization.

A wall surrounds the 50-foot-high citadel at Mohenjo-daro and apparently was intended to keep the inhabitants away from the city's "treasury," the state granary. This imposing structure had a floor area of about 9,000 square feet and sloping brick walls that gave it a fortress-like aspect. Other buildings on the citadel probably housed religious and secular officials, although one of them contained a large bath, which may have served a ritual function.

Below the citadel, the town spread out in a "gridiron" pattern, whose regularity suggests that the Indus civilization may have been the first to practice town planning. Several streets, each about 45 feet wide, cross at right angles. Branching off the streets are narrow lanes, giving access to the houses, along with the gridiron plan, give this part of the city a severe appearance.

Yet the citizens of Mohenjo-daro seem to have lived fairly well by ancient standards. Most of their houses had two stories and a ground floor area about 30 feet square. They contained courtyards and some modern conveniences, such as a bathroom and a toilet. An elaborate system of drains, lined and edged with brickwork and sometimes covered with stones, ran throughout the streets of the city.

As in other ancient cities, most of the people lived by farming, with wheat, barley, and cotton among the crops. They kept domesticated animals, including cattle, buffaloes, horses, and camels. Another source of income was trade. The Indus River and its tributaries served as arteries of commerce between cities. Some traders went even farther—across the mountains and desert to Afghanistan and Mesopotamia. Jewelry found in the Indus Valley shows marked similarities to some found in Mesopotamia and other parts of the Middle East. Some archaeologists have speculated that

the idea of the city may have spread to the Indus Valley from the Middle East, a belief that receives support from the evidence of trade between these areas.

About the same time that towns were beginning to appear in the Indus Valley, the peasant communities of northern China were undergoing a similar change in economy. By about 1500 B.C. the region included a few good-sized walled towns. The number of towns grew steadily, and by about 100 B.C. the majority of the population of 60 million people lived in towns and cities.

These northern Chinese towns seem to have been severely rectangular and dominated by walls. Each house was surrounded by a wall, which had only one gate. The houses were grouped in wards, which also had walls and only one entrance. Another rectangular wall enclosed the entire city.

Under the T'ang dynasty of emperors (A.D. 618 to 907), urban life reached a high degree of refinement, reflecting the wealth of the empire. The capital city of Ch'ang-an was one of the most splendid cities ever built anywhere. At the peak of its development in the 700s, a million people lived within its walls, with perhaps another million outside. The walled city covered 30 square miles. The massive outer wall, 18 feet high, had 12 gates, three on each side. The main one, the five-doored "Gate of Brilliant Virtue," was 150 feet wide. Inside, streets 225 feet wide ran east and west.

Even broader avenues, running north and south, measured 480 feet in width. At the end of the main avenue stood the walled Imperial City. Here were located the offices of the huge bureaucracy that governed the city and the empire.

Another walled enclosure contained palaces and ceremonial buildings belonging to the emperor, who was considered to be divine. He had many ceremonial duties, including the regular audiences attended by government officials. An early Chinese poet, Tu Fu, has described the atmosphere at one of these occasions:

This painting from the T'ang dynasty period of China provides some idea of the luxurious ceremony that must have attended great occasions in the capital city of Ch'ang-an. The artist has depicted a procession carrying a Buddhist deity in a chariot.

Outside the inner doors, the two court ladies
  with flowing purple sleeves
Now turn to the throne to lead the procession
  from the audience chamber
The spring wind blows the swirling smoke of
  incense in the hall
The sunlight plays across the dazzling robes
  of the thousand officials
We hear the striking of the hour from the
  clepsydra in the high tower
As a servitor standing near, I note that the
  Heavenly Countenance is joyful. . . .

In ancient Imperial China, the civil service
was a most desirable calling. Every year,
thousands of young men from all over
China poured into the city to take the state
examinations. Of those who qualified, many
were sent to provincial posts; and even those
lucky enough to be assigned to the capital
lived—for the most part—in comfortable
but modest circumstances. The few who
reached the top of the ladder lived sump-
tuously, as did the landed aristocrats.
Wealthy families vied with each other in
building increasingly lavish houses and
gardens. One high official achieved an early
form of air-conditioning: the roof of his
private pavilion was watered by a number
of fountains, thus creating a cool haven for a
hot summer day.

These great houses—like the simpler
ones—were constructed mainly of timber.
They seldom lasted more than a few generations. More permanent building materials,
such as baked brick, were used for the many
temples and pagodas that adorned the city.
One of these pagodas still stands today and is
virtually all that remains of Ch'ang-an.

The splendor of Ch'ang-an gradually declined along with the power of the T'ang
dynasty, and in the mid-800s it was destroyed by rebels. But Chinese urban traditions continued in other cities. When the
Venetian Marco Polo visited Peking in the
late 1200s, he marveled at the city's riches:

"Everything in the world that is rare and
precious finds its way to this city . . . precious
stones, pearls and spices which come from

India. All the valuable products of the
Chinese provinces are brought here to
satisfy the needs of the people. . . . 1,000
wagons and packhorses carrying nothing but
raw silk enter the city daily: and the gold-
encrusted materials and silks of all kinds are
manufactured here in staggering quantities."

Just as Marco Polo had been amazed by
the civilization of China, so other Europeans, the Spanish Conquistadors, were
surprised to find in America several thriving
urban cultures. One of Cortés's officers,
Bernal Diaz, described the market of the
Aztec capital Tenochtitlán, in these words:

". . . we were astonished at the crowds of
people, and the regularity which prevailed,
as well as the vast quantities of merchandise.
Each kind had its particular place, which
was distinguished by a sign. The articles
consisted of gold, silver, jewels, feathers . . .
chocolate, and great numbers of slaves,
some of whom were fastened by the neck, in
collars, to long poles. The meat market was
stocked with fowls, game, and dogs . . . and
the merchants who dealt in gold had the
metal in grains as it came from the mines,
in transparent tubes. . . . The entire square
was enclosed in colonnades. . . . Some of the
soldiers among us who had been in many
parts of the world, in Constantinople, and all
over Italy, and in Rome, said that so large a
market-place and so full of people, and so
well regulated and arranged, they had never
beheld before."

The population of Tenochtitlán at the
time of the conquistadors has been estimated at between 75,000 and 80,000—
greater than any city in Spain in those days.
The city stood on the site of the present
Mexico City. The land was originally

The Aztec capital of Tenochtitlán, shown in a map
made under the supervision of its Spanish conqueror
Cortés. The map shows the lake surrounding the city
and the causeways linking the city to the mainland.
At the center is the mile-square temple precinct (shown
enlarged), where the Aztecs made human sacrifices to
their gods of people conquered in their wars.

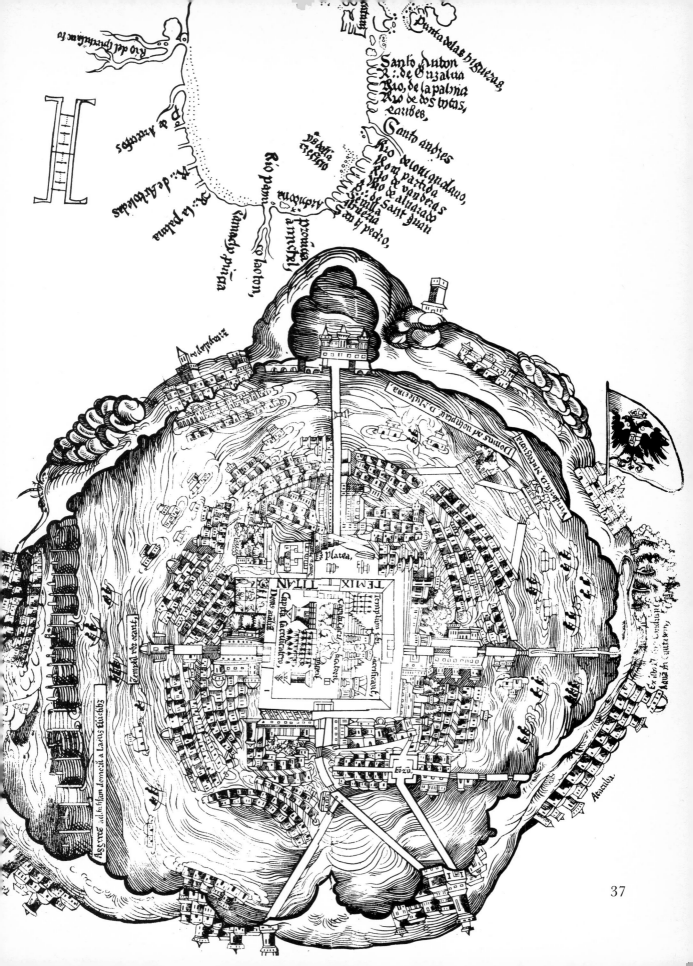

37

dotted with lakes, now mostly filled in. In the middle of one of these lakes was the island capital of the Aztec Empire. Four causeways connected it to the shore. One of these was so wide and strong, Cortés noted, "that eight horsemen could ride along it abreast." Because the lake water was undrinkable, the Aztecs built two great aqueducts to bring fresh water from springs on the mainland. Boats collected the city's waste, which was used as fertilizer.

Many of the streets of the island city were in fact canals, and nearly every household had its canoe. On land, four straight avenues led to the mile-square temple precinct in the center of the city. It contained several stepped pyramids, whose stairways were stained with blood.

This was the dark side of the Aztec civilization: a cruel and gory religion that required, to appease its gods, a regular supply of still-beating human hearts. The victims were usually conquered peoples.

A short distance from the scene of these ghastly rites, the subjects of the Emperor Moctezuma lived reasonably comfortable lives. Even the poorest of them had neat little houses, and many had gardens of vegetables and flowers. Cortés noted with approval the existence of public baths.

The rich lived in stone houses built around courtyards. The flat roofs of the houses served as terraces where one could enjoy the fresh cool air in the evening. Furnishings were simple. Even the wealthiest people slept on the floor on beds of matting. Such beds, with canopies, were provided for the Spaniards while they lived in the palace at Axycatl as guests of Moctezuma.

Eventually, the Spanish repaid this hospitality by laying siege to the city. They stamped out most of the Aztec civilization, destroyed Tenochtitlán, and superimposed their own culture on the land.

Before the Aztec empire flourished, several other civilizations had held sway in the Americas. Among these earlier cultures was that of the Mayas, a people who lived in

The cities built by the Maya Indians in Central America lay hidden in dense jungle for centuries. Their existence was revealed to the world in the mid-1800s by American archaeologist John L. Stephens, and artist Frederick Catherwood, whose drawings—at right, a temple in Tuluum—portray in meticulous detail the genius of the Maya builders.

The lost city of Machu Picchu, built by the Incas high in the Peruvian Andes, was never found by the Conquistadors. An American historian, Hiram Bingham, discovered it in 1911. Its terraces, temples, and palaces, constructed of granite blocks ingeniously wedged together without mortar, remain virtually intact.

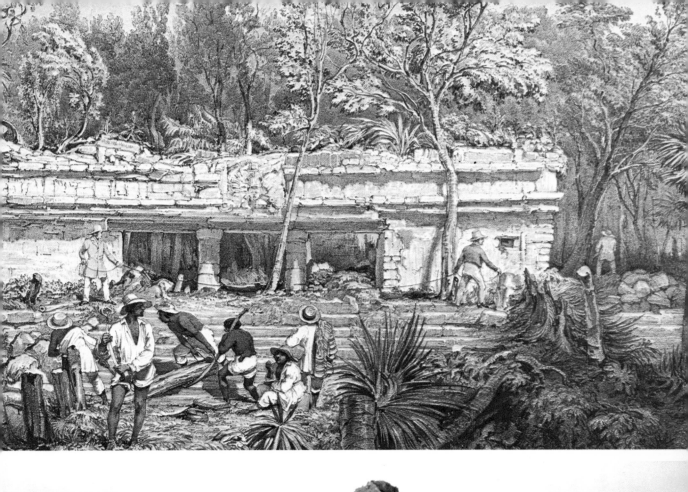

the Yucatán Peninsula of Mexico and in the northern parts of what we now call Central America. Several Mayan cities may have boasted populations of more than 200,000, though their "limits" merged imperceptibly into farming land. Their centers boasted a variety of immense stepped pyramids, some of which may have served as temples and altars and some as observatories from which priests made calculations for their calendars.

By the time the Spaniards had arrived, the Mayan civilization was in decline. But in Peru, the conquerors found another flourishing empire—that of the Incas. The Inca capital of Cuzco, high in the Andes, had much to impress the Spanish invaders. Great palaces and temples made of stone lined the main plaza. Some of the walls were plated with sheets of gold. Here the gold-hungry Spaniards found all the treasure they could have imagined.

Even more impressive, for its masterful engineering, was a city the Spaniards never found: Machu Picchu. This mountain city was built entirely of stones—the Incas were skilled masons. Its many terraces of buildings spread over 100 acres of precipitous rock. Still in a good state of preservation, Machu Picchu is an awe-inspiring example of human tenacity and ingenuity.

Today Machu Picchu is deserted. The civilization that built it is long dead—like many others whose cities are today no more than mounds of rubble.

But, as one urban culture declines, another evolves. We have seen that civilizations of Egypt and Mesopotamia faded. In their place arose, in turn, Athens and Rome. These civilizations also declined and were eclipsed by others, and their splendid buildings became ruins. But their languages, laws, philosophy, art, and architecture have profoundly influenced the world of western man. The way we speak and think, our ideas of justice, ethics, and beauty, would be very different without these two great cities.

Athens was one of many Greek city-states

that began to grow up around the Aegean Sea between 1000 and 500 B.C. The geography of this area—a group of scattered islands and a rocky mainland with an irregular coast—fostered the independent development of the Greek communities. The people relied for sustenance on relatively small plots of land, and their cities tended to have a rural atmosphere. Most of

the population of a Greek city (usually totaling about 10,000) were small farmers.

By the time Athens had reached the height of its power, in the 400s B.C., it had a free population of about 150,000, of whom half lived outside the walls. Of this free population, some 40,000 were full-fledged citizens, eligible to vote and take a direct part in the Athenian government. Some

100,000 slaves—mostly aliens—and about 20,000 free aliens made up the rest of the total population of 270,000.

Built on high ground five miles inland, Athens was linked to the sea and to a profitable sea-going trade by its port of Piraeus. A long defensive wall embraced the two cities. But the main defensive site and the ritual center of Athens was the Acropolis. This great rock towered over the rest of the city. Under the leadership of Pericles, a general who governed between 443 and 430 B.C., the Athenians crowned the Acropolis with one of the most beautiful groups of temples ever built. Chief among these was the Parthenon, dedicated to the goddess Athena. The Athenians did not depend on size to impress; the Parthenon, for example, measures only 230 feet long and 35 feet high. What impresses is the lofty site, the graceful symmetrical grouping of the buildings, and the sheer beauty of the buildings themselves.

Below the Acropolis, the rest of the ancient city spread out haphazardly, a con-

Left: The ruins of the Parthenon, built on the Acropolis in the fifth century B.C. Below: Set in the rough-hewn stone wall of the Parthenon (inside the columns), this doorway provides a view of modern Athens and, in the distance, the Attic hills.

fusion of rude houses separated by narrow and tortuous alleys, most of them unpaved and all of them used as garbage dumps and sewers. These were not the slums of Athens; the houses of rich and poor stood here side by side and were similar—except that those of the wealthy were larger and likely to be built of unbaked brick with a tiled roof, rather than of mud and twigs.

The Pompeiian taste for luxury is evident in this elaborate fountain in the courtyard of a rich Pompeiian's house. In some houses the ground floor was heated by a system of hot-air pipes, called hypocausts. The upper story generally served as slave quarters.

One of the well-preserved streets of Pompeii. The streets are paved with blocks of hard lava, and all of them are bordered by sidewalks. Small shops—including many wineshops—lined the streets. These were built into the front sections of some of the larger houses.

The city's water supply was limited, which partly explains the squalor of the streets. Some households had tanks or wells; others would send a slave with a jug or go themselves to the public fountains. These fountains were often dedicated to some god or hero and so were protected by superstition against defilement. Some of the Athenian houses may have had bathrooms, but in general the citizens preferred the more sociable public baths.

The main gathering place of the Athenians was the *agora*. This large open space served as market and as the social and political center of the city—its "crossroads." It was enclosed by municipal buildings and colonnades, and shaded by trees. A Greek poet, Eubolus, observed that:

"You will find everything sold together in the same place at Athens: figs, witnesses to summonses, bunches of grapes, turnips, pears, apples, givers of evidence, roses, porridge, honeycombs, chick-peas, law suits . . . irises, lamps, water-clocks, laws, indictments."

The port of Piraeus also had its agora, located near the harbor. This city's orderly planned streets contrasted sharply with the jumble that was Athens. Piraeus was one of the first planned cities in the western world. It was built by the Greek architect Hippodamus, a pupil of Pythagoras. His geometric training is apparent in the gridiron pattern, which he popularized. This rectangular planning must have appealed strongly to the intellectual Greeks, with their logical approach to the universe. When the opportunity came to build from scratch, they reveled in the grid pattern.

Greek ships sailed the Mediterranean, and Greek colonies sprang up around its shores, including parts of Italy. It may have been Greek influence that gave Pompeii its geometric street plan. This town was occupied in turn by several Italian peoples before it was taken over by the Romans in about 80 B.C.

In A.D. 79, the nearby volcano Mount Vesuvius erupted, burying Pompeii and some 2,000 of its inhabitants in molten lava. Excavations carried out during the past two centuries have uncovered most of Pompeii, which remains virtually intact. From its well-preserved houses, shops, and public buildings, we can get a clear idea of Roman city life in the early days of the Empire.

The name Pompeii brings luxury to mind, and in fact many of the Pompeians were rich. Their way of life is evoked by the many private houses left standing and partly restored. Mosaic floors, inlaid marble walls, and frescoes reveal the Pompeians' taste for decoration. In one house the table is still set for a lavish banquet; before it was served, apparently, the owner was forced to flee from the approaching lava. Most of the furnishings were destroyed in the eruption, although here and there a marble table, or an object such as a silver dish or a terra-cotta vase, has been recovered. But it is the houses themselves that offer the clearest indications of Pompeian life and of Roman ideas of comfort. The outer walls have few, if any, windows. Natural light comes from an inner courtyard, or *atrium*, whose roof has an opening to let in sunlight. The entrance hall may have inscribed on the floor a motto, "Profit is joy," or a warning, "Beware of

the dog." Close beside the atrium, which contains an altar to the household gods, are the various rooms, often including a private bath. In some houses there are two dining rooms—an enclosed one for the cooler months, and a summer one open to the sky.

The comfort of the wealthy Pompeian's house might also be found in the house of a patrician of Rome itself. But the Roman house was surrounded by very different kinds of dwellings. An inventory of all the buildings in Rome, compiled in A.D. 312-315, includes 1,790 mansions, and 46,602 apartment buildings.

These apartment houses—and not the luxurious mansions often thought of as typically Roman—housed the vast majority of the population. They appear to have been the first multistory dwellings in the ancient world. Like any crowded modern city, Rome was forced to build upward as well as outward. It could not spread out

nearly as much as the modern city can, because its people had to rely on their own two feet for transportation. They wanted to live within the city walls for protection and to be within walking distance of the forum, the baths, and the entertainments that Rome offered its citizens. And so they lived on top of each other.

Some of their apartment buildings—called *insulae*—were five stories high. But many of these were badly constructed; their walls were too thin to support the masonry. It was not unusual for an insula to collapse.

Rents were high and continually rising. To make ends meet, many tenants were forced to sub-let one or two rooms of their own apartment—resulting in severe overcrowding. The ground floors of some insulae were used for shops. In other buildings, a single tenant occupied a luxurious ground floor apartment.

45

The Romans were master engineers, as can be seen in the splendid Roman aqueducts still standing today. They built an elaborate system of sewers; one of these, the Cloaca Maxima, dates from the sixth century B.C. and was so large and well-made that it is still in use today. Unfortunately, the system served only those people who lived in private houses and on the ground floors of the insulae. Those who lived above used either public toilets or covered cisterns kept in the building. Similarly, a private piped-in water supply, including a private bath, was

an amenity restricted to the rich. The poor carried their water from public wells. Wealthy Romans' houses were equipped with a form of central heating on the ground floor. When the poor were cold—and a Roman winter can be chilly—they closed the shutters, plunging the room into darkness, except for the dim light of an oil lamp.

To escape temporarily from these congested, inadequate quarters, the Roman could make his way through the equally congested streets to partake of some of Rome's public amenities. He could visit one of the many parks or open squares. In the forum, he could forget the sordid realities of his own living conditions while gazing at

A visitor to modern Rome will find many traces of the splendor of the ancient city. The crumbling monuments and temples of the forum (shown above, with a Renaissance church in the background) evoke the pomp and ceremony of the Empire, while the great Colosseum (right and far right) recalls the blood-thirsty crowds—and those who died to entertain them.

Roman achievements in
architecture and
engineering can be found
throughout Europe.
Left: The graceful arches
of the Pont du Gard, a
Roman aqueduct near
Nîmes, in southern France.

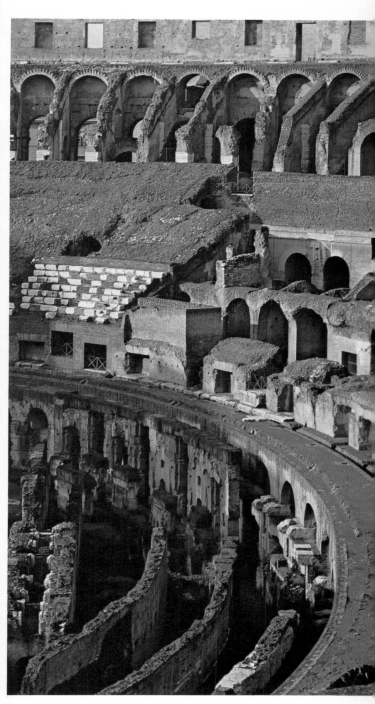

the magnificent temples, archways, and monuments that symbolized imperial glory and power. Here, as in the Greek agora, were markets and places to do business. But the forum also served as "acropolis" and included a number of temples to the Roman gods. Its spacious layout allowed great crowds to watch imperial processions and other important public occasions. The Romans built on a grand scale. Whereas the Greeks had been restricted to the lintel (a horizontal beam), the Romans developed the arch and the dome, which enabled them to span large areas. The ruins of the Forum and other ancient buildings and monuments scattered around Rome still impress the beholder. Although most of ancient Rome was a chaotic mass of tenements and narrow streets—reflecting the city's origin as a group of villages—the parts built by the government to glorify the state were open and admirably planned to accommodate large numbers of people.

Near the forum stands the Colosseum. This vast arena could hold 45,000 people; the Circus Maximus (no longer standing) may have held as many as 385,000. Hungry for diversions, the people flocked to such arenas and theaters to watch the spectacles provided for them by the rulers. Sometimes the entertainment took the form of plays, chariot races, games, horse racing, or innocuous animal tricks like those in circuses today. Increasingly, though, the Romans demanded more cruel entertainments. Gladiators fought to the death. Or—for more jaded appetites—an armed man slaughtered one who was unarmed, and was then disarmed himself and killed by another.

A more civilized Roman institution was the bath. Romans took bathing seriously. More than just a way of getting clean, it was a process of refreshing the skin, toning the body, and reviving one's spirit. A typical public bath contained a whole series of baths—hot, tepid, and bracingly cold. Steam baths and exercise and massage rooms were available. Even facilities not normally associated with bathing, such as shops,

libraries, and academies, were attached to the larger baths.

The Roman life style and the Roman city followed its armies through most of western Europe. The bath, the arena, and the forum appeared in modified forms in Spain, France, and England.

Provincial Roman towns were much smaller than the capital. Verulamium (the largest town in Roman Britain after London—or Londinium, as it was called) had a population of only about 5,000. All its inhabitants lived in one-family houses—

These bas-reliefs depict everyday life in ancient Rome. Above: A Roman blacksmith's shop. Left: A butcher's shop; note the cleaver, very similar to the kind used by butchers today, and the basin for the unsaleable parts of the carcass. The customer is apparently sitting and waiting for her order.

some little more than huts, others luxurious villas. Despite its small size, Verulamium was an important urban center: a seat of government and a market for the surrounding region. Like most Roman towns, it had impressive public buildings, including several temples, a town hall, and a large theater that may have accommodated the whole population.

Verulamium, and the other Roman towns throughout Europe, flourished for a few hundred years. Then, as Rome declined, its provincial outposts declined also. Populations dwindled until the towns lost all semblance of urban life. Verulamium became a village within the rubble of its Roman wall. In Rome itself, the Emperor Diocletian's palace was occupied by peasants. Throughout Europe, the idea of the city—and civilization—lay dormant.

Right: The ruins of the Roman theater at Verulamium, north of London. An important city under the Romans, Verulamium declined, and was succeeded by St. Albans in the Middle Ages.

Left: A model of a five-story apartment house of ancient Rome. The ground floor of such a building normally consisted of spacious apartments for rich tenants; the upper floors had more modest quarters. The walls of these buildings were generally too thin to support the floors, and some of them collapsed.

The Medieval City

3

Bruges in winter. One of the many bridges that gave the city its Flemish name, "Brugge," spans the still water of a canal. During medieval times, this city was a thriving center of international trade and a cultural capital of the first rank. Walking along its canals and narrow cobbled streets today, one can gain a sense of what it may have been like to live in a medieval town.

TODAY, the canals of Bruges, in Belgium, are used mainly by swans and sightseeing boats. Five hundred years ago, these canals would have been filled with barges loaded with merchandise from all over Europe. In its prime, Bruges was one of Europe's main trading centers—almost on a par with Venice. Its active commercial and cultural life are representative of the flowering of European cities after the fall of Rome.

The prosperity of Bruges had begun with the development of the weaving industry in Flanders in the 12th century. The quality of Flemish woolen cloth began to attract merchants from other countries, who brought other commodities to trade. An overland trade route, linking Bruges with Venice, helped to stimulate commerce and put northern Europe in closer touch with the Mediterranean.

The city's great stroke of luck came in the form—ironically—of a tidal wave. In the early 1100s (probably 1134), a great wave cut through the silt of the narrow channel that linked Bruges to the sea, and turned part of the channel into a large harbour. After that, the city's international trade increased many times over. By the 1400s, the number of ships using the harbor had declined slightly, owing to the gradual silting-up of the channel. But even then it was not unusual for 150 or more ships to sail into the harbor in a single day. Once the ships were anchored, their goods would be transferred to barges and carried up the canal through a series of locks and into the city.

On the quays of Bruges, men would be busy unloading the goods: great sacks of English wool to be woven into cloth by the

51

This map of Bruges shows the city in the 1500s, after its decline as a commercial center. At the left is the estuary that linked Bruges to its harbor. Notice the double moat and the seven fortified gates into the city. At the center is the Grand' Place and the Belfry.

BRVGÆ, *vulgo* Brugk, Teutonicæ Flandriæ vrbs omnium pulcherrima, nitidissimaq, publicarum siquidem, priuatarumq ædium in hac vrbe splendor & magnificentia, omnem rationem, omnem dicendi facultatem superat. Optimam vrbium formam, hoc est, orbicularem, situ obtinet, aquis probè in

Flemish weavers, pepper and spices from the Orient, carpets from Turkey. Heavy items, such as kegs of Rhenish wine, or live pigs from Denmark, would be unloaded with the help of the town crane. This large and ingenious machine was operated by means of two great wheels in which men walked as on a treadmill. It was in constant use from morning until evening.

Bruges was a cosmopolitan city. Most of the countries trading there maintained permanent representatives in the city, and some of them had consulates in the city. There was, for example, a large English community established around the Place St. Jean, where the English had their own church and their own inn, the Inghelsche Herberghe. In the 1400s the merchant and printer William Caxton was Governor of the English merchants in Bruges. Here, he set up a printing press and published the first book printed in English, *The Recuyell of the Historyes of Troyes*.

The wealth of the Bruges merchants and of the dukes of Burgundy (who acquired the city by marriage in 1384) attracted the finest artists in northern Europe. Among the painters working in Bruges in the 1400s were such masters as Hans Memling and Jan van Eyck—one of the first to develop the technique of painting in oils rather than in tempera. Besides painting the religious scenes that were the main subjects of medieval art, they also portrayed prominent citizens and the interiors of their homes.

Civic pride was expressed in the construction of many beautiful buildings, including the ornate town hall, the various guilds' houses, and the Belfry, which rises 350 feet up from the Grand' Place, or market square. Graceful stone bridges—from which the city takes its Flemish name, Brugge—crossed the canals. A Spanish nobleman visiting the city in the 1430s commented on the "fine houses and streets . . . very beautiful churches and monasteries and excellent inns."

"The people," he continued, "are . . . very extravagant in their food, and much given to all kinds of luxury." They were especially fond of pageants and festivals. The fact that these were nearly always tied to some religious observance didn't prevent them from being lively and colorful. In the most famous festival, the Procession of the Holy Blood, the town jester marched along with the priests and other notables, entertaining the crowds with his tricks.

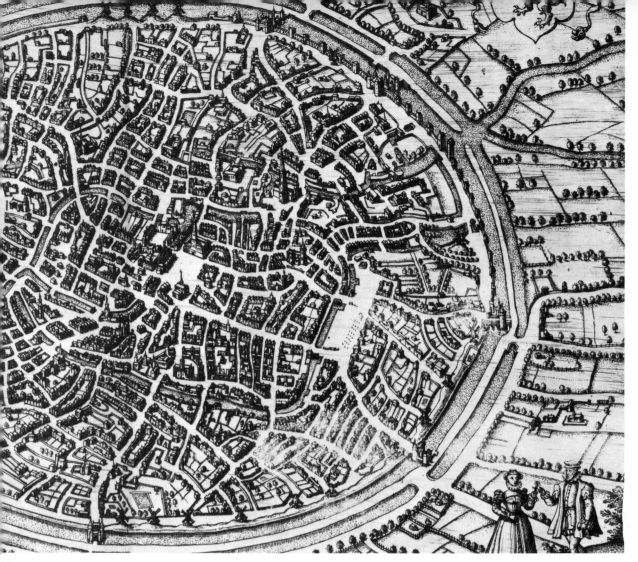

The year 1430 saw one of the most splendid festivals in the city's history, the celebration of the marriage of Duke Philip the Good to Isabella of Portugal. An elaborate procession to welcome the new duchess included 100 trumpeters, as well as nobles, priests, and merchants, and made its way through streets hung with tapestries, past fountains running with wines or perfumes. For two weeks, the citizens of Bruges celebrated the marriage with games, plays, and jousting in the Grand' Place. In the city's numerous inns, thousands of barrels of beer were consumed.

Bruges was a merry and prosperous city, but it was also a violent one. Political strife broke out over and over again. Within a year of the joyous celebration of Philip and Isabella's wedding, the duke's soldiers were fighting the townspeople in the streets. The Flemish were fierce fighters, but ultimately the duke triumphed and promptly took bloody revenge on his enemies. Public executions were a common sight in Bruges. These were carried out—often with extreme cruelty—in the Grand' Place. Severed heads were displayed on the Belfry.

Apart from human cruelty, many accidents and diseases continually afflicted people in the Middle Ages. From the top of the Belfry fire wardens kept watch for outbreaks of fire; but even this vigilance did not prevent 1,500 houses from being burned down in the year 1413 alone. Famines, too, occurred from time to time. In common with all people living in Europe in those days,

the citizens of Bruges suffered severe outbreaks of diseases for which there were as yet no cures; dysentery, leprosy, tuberculosis, and smallpox were among the most deadly. Bruges was very badly hit by the Black Death, a form of bubonic plague that swept through Europe in the mid-1300s.

Surrounded by all the commercial activity, the merry-making, and the brutality of everyday life in Bruges were a number of quiet retreats—monasteries and convents in whose cloistered gardens men and women could practice the spiritual life. Among the loveliest of these was—and is—the Béguinage, located near the city wall. It offered shelter for women who did not wish to take vows, but who wanted to live under the protection of the Church.

Seen against the busy life of Bruges, a monastery appears a contradiction of urban values—"in" the world, but not "of" it. And yet the Church, and the religious houses in particular, played a major part in the slow rebirth of western European cities after centuries of disorder. A thriving city such as Bruges was the culmination of a long, halting process of re-civilization.

Although many factors contributed to the rise of medieval cities, the Church is perhaps a good one to consider first, because it was the only institution to survive the gradual takeover of the western Roman Empire by barbarian peoples. From the 400s onwards, the Roman administrative network fell apart. The complex system of Roman law broke down. Long-distance trade began to decline, and by the 700s had nearly disappeared. But the Christian Church remained. Its bishops were established in the cities founded by the Romans, and most remained there throughout the following centuries, even after the civic life of these towns had dwindled to practically nothing.

54

Left: Bruges as it looked in the late 1400s—a detail from *The Virgin of the Rose Garden* by an anonymous Flemish painter. Two of the city's landmarks are the Church of Notre Dame (far left) and the Belfry. The mountains are imaginary. Above: A modern view of medieval Bruges.

Right: The Bruges town crane in operation, hoisting kegs of wine or beer from a barge. The work was done by the men walking the great wheel. In the foreground, some prosperous merchants are conducting business.

In his cathedral town, or "see," a bishop would retain a number of assistant clerics to help him conduct services and administer the diocese. There might be a school for the training of priests, and a monastery. A few craftsmen and merchants supplied the clerical households with goods. Amid all the chaos of these "Dark Ages"—the fighting, the migrations, the invasions of Moors and Vikings—the Church carried on its work. It managed to convert most of the barbarian peoples of western Europe. Its authority transcended the divisions of tribe, race, and language. Priests and monks scattered all over Europe were linked not only by their faith, but also by the organization of the Church, by a common language—Latin—and by the body of learning they preserved.

Outside the Church, nearly everyone was illiterate. Even Charlemagne, crowned Holy Roman Emperor in the year 800, never quite mastered writing, although he could read a little. He did, however, encourage a revival of learning and an increase in the number of manuscripts copied—both biblical and classical.

Unfortunately, this flowering was quickly cut down in the 900s by new waves of invasions, chiefly by the Norsemen, or Vikings, who did not hesitate to destroy a great number of monasteries and everything in them, except for items of monetary value. Attacked by Vikings from the north, Moors from Africa, and Slavs and Magyars from the east, the fledgling civilization of western Europe seemed doomed. Charlemagne's empire had split into pieces after his death, and his successors were generally ineffectual against the invaders.

Left: This round tower in County Wicklow, Ireland, once protected Christians from the fury of the Viking invaders. Irish monks produced some of the most beautiful, elaborately illustrated manuscripts to be found in any civilization.

Right: By the time this engraving was made in the 15th century, European civilization was in full flower. Its survival during the Dark Ages was due in large part to the monks who preserved the store of learning inherited from the Roman Empire.

Under continual danger, the mass of the people depended on whatever security their feudal lord could offer. In return for the protection of his castle and his soldiers, they worked his land and yielded to him part of its produce. The peasants were also required to perform various services for the lord, such as doing maintenance work on his castle.

During this period, long-distance trade was nearly at a standstill. Earlier, western Europe had benefited from its trade with Constantinople (now Istanbul), capital of the Byzantine empire. This eastern empire was the successor to the Roman empire, and Constantinople was the center of a flourishing civilization while western Europe was struggling to survive. It was the hub of the great land routes to the Middle East, and its harbor attracted ships from all over the Mediterranean. Some western ports, such as Marseilles and Barcelona, had been sustained by their commerce with Constanti-

nople and other Mediterranean ports. In turn, they had stimulated inland trade.

In the 700s, the Moslems gained control of almost the whole of Spain and a considerable area of southern France. Such ports as Barcelona and Marseilles could no longer serve as trade links between western Europe and Constantinople. With the Mediterranean trade curtailed, western Europe was thrown back upon its own resources, which at that time were pitifully small.

The picture of western Europe in the 900s is that of a collection of small agrarian communities. Villagers paid their taxes to the feudal lord and provided for their own needs on a primitive level, always with one eye anxiously scanning the horizon for the sail of a Viking ship coming up the river. As the year 1000 approached, many people fearfully anticipated the end of the world.

The year 1000 came and went. Life proceeded as before. But very slowly changes

were beginning to take place in Europe. The Viking raids declined and stopped. Many of the Norse invaders settled down, became Christians, and took up farming. And although outbreaks of fighting continued to occur, there seemed to be a greater sense of security and optimism in the air. We can see evidence of this in the burst of artistic energy of the times, and in the gradual reestablishment of cities.

An early sign that a new Europe was taking shape was that the population began to grow. This growth was linked to a food surplus, which had resulted from a series of agricultural innovations. One of these was the introduction of the three-field system in the 700s. Formerly, peasants had divided their land into two fields, planting one with winter wheat and letting the other lie fallow. Now, they divided it into three fields. One

they planted in the autumn with winter wheat; another they planted in the spring with some other grain or vegetable; and the third they let lie fallow. Crops were rotated from one field to the next. With more land under cultivation at any given time, and more varied crops, the peasantry had a more substantial and better-balanced diet.

This and other improved farming techniques meant that more food could be produced by fewer workers. So people began to move to the towns—or, rather, to those settlements, both Roman and recently founded, that seemed to promise a better life than the average village could offer.

For one thing, a town offered security. Most towns had fortified walls, although this was less often the case in England than on the Continent. Many had the additional protection of a castle. Towns that grew up around a fortress were often known as "burghs," or "bourgs," or some other variation of that word, depending on the language of the country. The Austrian city of Salzburg, for example, was the "burg" on the Salzach River. Strasbourg, Edinburgh, and Canterbury are among the many other towns whose names reflect the defensive aspect of the medieval city.

Some burghs were established by feudal lords; others were founded by kings. Salzburg was among those founded and governed by the Church; the lords of its castle of Hohensalzburg were prince-archbishops. Ecclesiastical government gave a city a certain advantage. Whereas a secular lord often moved around from one castle to another, a bishop or abbot remained in his city all the time. Being permanently resident in the city, he gave it prestige as well as protection.

As a great landowner, the Church profited from the agricultural surplus, and its prosperity also helped the cities. The abbey of St. Alban, one of the richest religious establishments in England, stood near the old Roman city of Verulamium. Soon after being rebuilt in the late 900s, the abbey founded three new parish churches and established a market. The old Roman road, Watling Street, which had run through Verulamium, was deflected to pass by the abbey's doors. Here, the new market was set up. Travelers, traders, and the abbey itself benefited from the commerce. This market was the genesis of the city of St. Albans. In other European cities, this pattern was repeated. We can see it today in the shops that still cluster around the walls of many European churches. In medieval times, the Church commanded the respect of the entire population, and even thieves and ruffians would not violate its premises. The security enjoyed by the Church extended to the markets it established. Where a market was located away from the church, a cross was erected in the marketplace as a reminder of ecclesiastical protection.

Although its elegant palaces and churches give Salzburg a mainly baroque aspect, this Austrian city is of medieval origin, and the gray fortress on the hill, once home of a succession of prince-archbishops, formerly dominated the city in a political sense, as well as visually.

Whereas most towns' commerce consisted of weekly markets, offering local produce and crafts, a few cities held large international fairs that lasted several weeks and attracted merchants from great distances. The French city of Troyes, for example, was host to two of the great fairs of the province of Champagne, the "Hot" Fair of St. Jean, held in July and August, and the "Cold" Fair of St. Rémi, held in November and December. The merchants who flocked to these fairs from all over Europe would leave after a few weeks, but during that time business boomed. Like a modern business convention, a medieval trade fair was a great financial asset to a city. Even though the population declined between fairs, the occasional international trade promoted city growth over a long period of time. The resident population of merchants and craftsmen increased. A middle class—the "burghers" or "bourgeoisie"—began to emerge. A few of these people amassed fortunes. In fact, part of a poem by Chrétien de Troyes translates: "At Bar, at Provins, or at Troyes, one can't help getting rich."

Today, ambitious young people all over the world gravitate to the cities, because that's where things are happening. To a young peasant living in medieval Europe, the nearest town must have had a similar attraction. It might be very small—a mere village by modern standards—but things were happening there. A man had opportunities.

There was the alluring possibility of eventually becoming a rich merchant. In the meantime, a youth could apprentice himself to a craftsman and become a weaver, a silversmith, or a wheelwright. The building boom caused by the growing population promised plenty of work for carpenters and stonemasons. An apprentice stonemason might have to start by helping to repair the old Roman wall around the city, or building a new wall, but when he became a master of his craft, he might undertake more challenging jobs. He might work on

The Italians seem always to have had a love of cities and a flair for building them. Italian painters have left many colorful representations of life in their cities—among them, Ambrogio Lorenzetti's *The Effects of Good Government in City and Country*, which depicts prosperous citizens and farmers from the outlying area, engaged in peaceful commerce and friendly visiting.

the vaults and buttresses of the city's new cathedral, or even carve the statues of saints and kings that would adorn its façade.

Perhaps the most immediate attraction of

the town—for a serf, at least—was freedom. Once he had lived there for a certain length of time—usually a year and a day—he would be released from his feudal obligations. He might come and go as he chose.

The feudal landlord was glad enough to see a city develop within his domain and to give it a charter. He could afford to grant the inhabitants a certain amount of political independence in return for the rents and

taxes he could gain from them. Their prosperity increased his own. The serfs who remained on the land continued to provide him with a share of the harvest and to maintain his estates, and the additional revenue he obtained from the cities could make him a very rich man.

While western European cities were slowly beginning to grow, other parts of the world had flourishing urban civilizations. Constantinople may have had 1 million people. It had splendid palaces, squares, avenues, and churches, including the great cathedral Hagia Sophia, whose vast dome spanned an area of 8,800 square feet.

In the Middle Ages, Spain belonged to the Moors, an Islamic people originally from North Africa. The Moors built several magnificent cities in Spain. Córdoba had

many dazzling and colorful mosques and palaces, a few of which are still standing. The palace of Alhambra, in Granada, gives us a good idea of Moorish luxury and delight in ornamentation. These buildings, with their brilliant mosaics and lacy grilles, obviously belong to a different culture from that evolving north of the Pyrenees. They were part of the world of Islam.

Elsewhere around the Mediterranean, the Islamic empire built other great cities, such as Cairo and Damascus. But the greatest of these cities was the capital of the empire, Baghdad, whose population may have reached a million. Its caravanserai (inns accommodating whole caravans) numbered in the thousands.

Church-building offered more scope for decoration. The 14th-century choir of Ely Cathedral shows the splendid, intricate work of medieval stonemasons and woodcarvers (the screen is Victorian). The pride of Ely is the Octagon and Lantern Tower (partly visible at top), a daring achievement of medieval engineering. Eight stone vaults support the tower—with the help of flying buttresses on the outside—spanning a width of 74 feet.

The Far East also had some great cities. The splendor of Chinese civilization was discovered in the 1200s by a Venetian, Marco Polo. His own city was prosperous and beautiful. But according to Marco Polo's accounts of his travels (even allowing for his tendency to exaggerate) it must have seemed almost provincial compared to the cities of China. He called Hangchow "the first and most splendid city in the world." It had 10 principal markets, each half a mile square. Each of its dozen guilds had more than 1,000 workshops, and each of these employed between 10 and 40 workers. "As for the merchants," said Marco Polo, "they are so many and so rich and handle such quantities of merchandise that no one could give a true account of the matter: it is so utterly beyond reckoning."

Compared to Islamic and Oriental cities, the western European cities of the early Middle Ages must have seemed very primitive. They were, to begin with, rather small. In 1086, London, the largest city in England, had only 20,000 people. Medieval European cities also lacked the monumental quality of many eastern cities; but they did have some splendid buildings. The castles around which many of them grew up are impressive structures. They may have offered little in the way of comfort, but were admirably suited to their main function: defense.

Yet it is the great churches that most clearly reveal the energy, skill, and confidence of this growing civilization. One has only to look at the massive columns, the high vaulting, the ingenious and graceful flying buttresses, and the brilliant stained-glass windows to appreciate the skill and taste of the medieval builders. Most of the craftsmen's names have been lost, but a few have come down to us. When the Norman conquerors of England wanted to rebuild Canterbury Cathedral, they sent for a French architect, William of Sens, whose work on the Cathedral of Sens had attracted favorable notice.

Even in those days, when travel was tedious and often dangerous, many people managed to get around and see what was happening in other cities. Lines of communication were opening up. Traders, pilgrims, and craftsmen brought back to their own cities ideas, news, techniques, and fashions from distant places. Urban life, even in the early Middle Ages, was beginning to be cosmopolitan.

Then, as now, many of the travelers and expatriates were students. Wandering scholars went from one abbey or cathedral school to another, discussing questions of philosophy and theology with respected teachers. In time, certain places acquired a more or less permanent community of scholars. From such beginnings, the medieval university developed.

The first of these was the University of Bologna, established in 1100. It was entirely student-run. The student council and rector not only handled the administration of the school, the renting of the lecture rooms, the selling of books, and other practical matters, but also hired and fired the professors.

Most of the students at Bologna studied law or medicine. Those at the University of Paris, founded in 1150, studied mainly philosophy and theology, as well as the other liberal arts and sciences. The University of Paris (where a teachers' guild—not students—was firmly in control) had a tremendous impact upon Europe. Scholars came to it from all over the Continent and England. Some of its English students went home and founded Oxford University. Other European universities were also offshoots of the one at Paris. One historian states that between 1150 and 1350 there was hardly a single eminent scholar in Europe who had not studied or taught in Paris.

Right: The building of Solomon's temple, as imagined by a medieval artist, Jean Fouquet. This miniature conveys some of the immense labor of constructing a gothic cathedral. In the foreground, masons carve and join great blocks of stone, while on the roof other workmen are engaged in gilding the façade—presumably to suggest the splendor of the temple.

Left: Montefrío, a hill town in southern Spain. Like most medieval towns it is dominated by its castle and church. This part of Spain was held by the Moors for nearly 800 years.

Enrollment had reached 6,000 by the 1200s.

The university was one of the main factors that made Paris the greatest city in medieval Europe. Trade, of course, was another, and the Church yet another. The city was also the home of the Capet family, who had become kings of France toward the end of the 900s. France at that time was considerably smaller than it is now. Even so, the French king was one of the most powerful rulers in Europe, and his capital had a corresponding prestige. King Philip Augustus, who reigned from 1180 to 1223, was responsible for most of the building of the medieval capital. He surrounded the city with high ramparts and built the first palace of the Louvre. Offended by the stench of the streets, he had them paved with cobbles.

In England, as in France, the monarchy was becoming stronger. Kings were expanding their domains, and in newly conquered territories, they found it prudent to establish new towns. These invaders' strongpoints are called "bastide" towns. One of the most active royal town-builders was King Edward I of England. Having conquered much of Wales in the late 13th century, Edward built a number of bastide towns. The army of workmen that he employed to build Flint in 1277 included 330 carpenters, 200 masons, and more than 1,200 diggers. Flint—like the other Welsh towns built by Edward at Caernarvon, Conway, and Beaumaris—was essentially a colonial town, a small pocket of Englishmen to control the unruly Welsh.

The English king also owned a huge chunk of southern France. Here, Edward built more bastide towns. The finest example of these is Montpazier, built in 1284. It was planned on a rigid grid scheme that divided the area inside the rectangular walls into 20 spaces. Of these lots, 18 were devoted to houses, one to the church, and one to an arcaded marketplace.

The grid pattern, which became very popular with builders of bastide towns, was particularly well-suited to the flat country of the Netherlands, where a number of Dutch nobles built bastides to assert their dominance over their land. Town-planning was

more common in Holland than in other parts of Europe. Much of the land itself was, in a sense, "planned"—that is, it had to be drained and built up, and thus gradually reclaimed from the sea. The development of towns, like the development of the land, was not left to chance.

In Italy, people took advantage of hilltops to build towns that would have a certain amount of natural resistance to enemy attack. Protection was supremely important, for the Italian city-states were continually at war with one another during the Middle Ages. When fighting did reach the city streets, the people took themselves to the towers. The town of San Gimignano was famous for its many towers, some of them nearly 350 feet high.

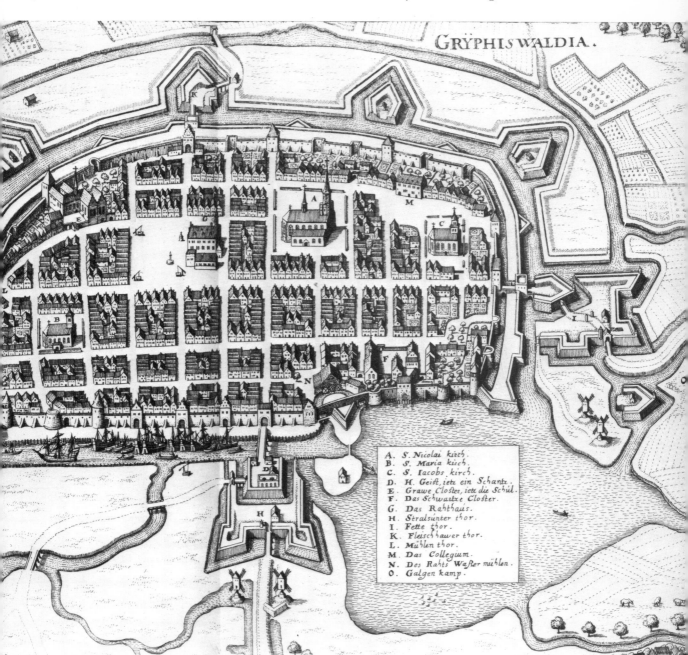

GRYPHISWALDIA.

A. S. Nicolai kirch.
B. S. Maria kirch.
C. S. Iacobs kirch.
D. H. Geist, iezt ein Schantz.
E. Grawe Closter, iezt die Schul.
F. Das Schwartze Closter.
G. Das Rahthaus.
H. Stralsunter thor.
I. Fette thor.
K. Fleischhawer thor.
L. Mühlen thor.
M. Das Collegium.
N. Des Rahts Waßer mühlen.
O. Galgen kamp.

Above: The town of San Gimignano in northern Italy, showing some of the medieval towers still standing. These towers were very useful during the intermittent wars conducted by Italian city-states against one another. They also had a symbolic value: wealthy nobles and merchants built them on their palaces partly to proclaim their power.

Left: Rothenburg-ob-der-Tauber in Bavaria looks like a stage set for a dramatized Grimms' fairy tale. Beautifully preserved, with much of its wall still intact, it gives visitors some idea of a German town of the Middle Ages.

Right: A street in the village of Riquewihr, in the wine-growing region of Alsace. The narrowness and irregularity of medieval streets give such towns much of their charm. Visual surprises lie behind every turn, and the crowding together of the houses creates a feeling of warmth and intimacy.

With the exception of the bastide towns, most medieval cities had a charming irregularity, which many modern city planners are beginning to copy. Apparently without any conscious intention, the medieval town builders used space in a way that was both practical and pleasing. The pedestrian is led around a corner into an open marketplace, then back through a twisting lane to an inn built around a courtyard or a church with a little plot of grass beside it. Every street beckons and promises. The scale is human. The houses, whether made of timber, stone, or brick, usually have a simplicity that heightens the effect of those few buildings on which wealth was lavished: the guildhalls, churches, town hall, and the residence of the prince, lord, or bishop.

Today, the streets of medieval cities such as Bruges are very congested, for the simple reason that they were not built for wheeled traffic. Almost everyone in a medieval town traveled on foot. The street was really just a space between houses.

When population increased sharply within the city walls, houses tended to become narrower and taller. In Nuremberg frontages were as small as 13 feet. The streets were little more than gutters. Edinburgh's Old

Town became very crowded within its wall, and people began to build high tenements. As in ancient Rome, the population moved up, rather than out.

Paris, which became the largest city in medieval Europe, rebuilt its wall five times between the 9th and the 12th century in order to accommodate its growing population. By the end of the 1100s it had a population of 100,000. A hundred years later it had grown to a quarter of a million, surpassing Venice, Bruges, and Milan.

The density of population in medieval towns and cities varied greatly. In some cases, the population did not grow as much as had been anticipated, and even within the city wall there were gardens, orchards, and cultivated fields. In the early 1300s the poet Petrarch wrote from the city of Palma, "I have a country house in the middle of a town and the town in the middle of the fields." This close connection with the countryside was very common in England, where walls rarely intervened between town and country, and it could still be felt on the eve of the Industrial Revolution. Its spirit is captured by Thomas Hardy in his description of the town of "Casterbridge" (Dorchester):

"The farmer's boy could sit under his barley-mow and pitch a stone into the office window of the Town clerk; reapers at work among the sheaves nodded to acquaintances on the pavement corner. Wheat ricks overhung the old Roman street, and green thatched barns opened directly upon the main thoroughfare."

Whether its density was high or low, the typical medieval town was small enough in area for people to be likely to encounter their acquaintances during the day.

Most people worked in or near their homes. The ground floor of a typical burgher's house would be his place of business—a shop, with perhaps a workshop and storerooms behind it. Going to work was simply a matter of going downstairs. For others it would be, at most, a few minutes'

walk. The medieval town had to remain compact because most people had had no other way of getting about than by walking.

The privacy so valued by modern western man was very scarce in the medieval city. Houses were small in relation to the number of people who lived and worked in them. Several poor families might live crowded together in one small house—as they still do today. But even a prosperous family would share its three- or four-story home with apprentices and servants. One large room, usually on the first floor above the shop, served the household as kitchen, dining room, and living room. This was generally the only room in the house that was heated. At bedtime, very few people had a private room to go to. Children and servants commonly slept in the same room with the master and mistress. Only gradually did the idea of the importance of privacy develop among the aristocracy and filter down to the middle classes. Its achievement, then and now, has depended on affluence and the size of families. Today's mushrooming urban populations once more make privacy increasingly difficult to obtain. This is one of the problems confronting architects and city planners. But there is little sign that the medieval town-dweller considered the lack of privacy a problem. Even where there was plenty of space within the walls, people chose to live crowded together. The family and the community represented security, which must have been—for a young civilization possibly still threatened with periodic violence—the most desirable quality in life.

Lack of privacy extended even to bathing. People used public bath houses, and in some towns both sexes shared the same facilities. The Spanish nobleman Tafur, who visited Bruges in 1438, was amazed by its mixed bathing, "which they take to be as honest as church-going is with us."

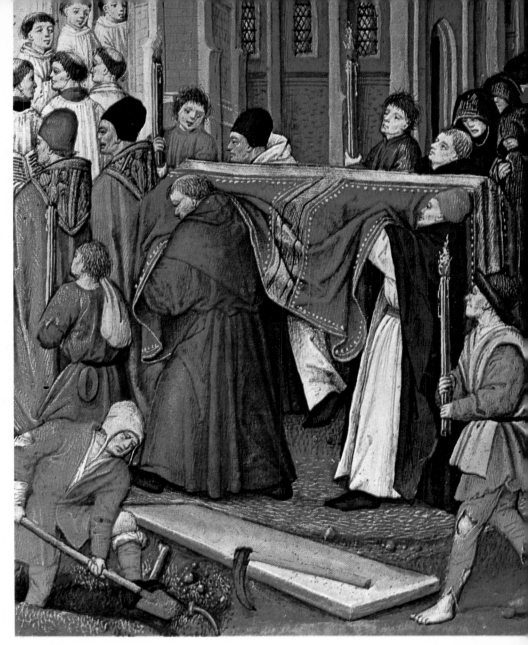

Left: *Visiting the Sick*, by the unknown Master of Alkmaar, in the Netherlands. One of a series called "The Seven Works of Mercy," the painting doubtless idealizes medieval charity, but it is interesting for its detail. The patient in the background is being bathed.

Right: This miniature from a 15th-century French Book of Hours shows a funeral procession. Notice the ragged clothes of the candle-bearers. Bones from earlier burials are being unearthed by the gravedigger. In the later Middle Ages, people were very preoccupied with the decay of the body.

Water for drinking and cooking was commonly obtained from public fountains. These were often ornamental as well as useful. As in ancient cities, the fountain became a meeting place where people could pass the time of day and rest from their chores. Along with the tavern, the area around the fountain was a major center for the exchange of news and gossip.

Running water was not available in private houses until the 1600s, and then it was provided by private companies and not by the city government. Waste disposal was,

of course, primitive. Where population density was low and houses had gardens behind them, it was possible to provide outhouses at a reasonable distance from the living quarters. Wastes could be removed to the nearby countryside and used as fertilizer. But even with plenty of open space in and around the city, odors could be most unpleasant. The presence in a Cambridge street of a large dung pile, which was carted away only once a week, may have been what prompted the English parliament meeting in that city in 1388 to pass the country's first urban sanitary law. It prohibited the throwing of garbage and wastes into ditches and waterways. Very often, medieval water supplies were polluted. But the evidence suggests that medieval sanitation was no worse than in many 19th-century cities.

The lack of disinfectants and the costliness of soap made very thorough house-cleaning impossible. When cities became more and more crowded, and many houses and tenements were inadequately ventilated, infectious diseases were more easily transmitted. Lack of sanitation was a major cause of the high infant mortality. A generally unbalanced diet, deficient in fresh fruit and vegetables, made people prone to scurvy. Cold, damp houses helped to precipitate many a case of pneumonia. Medieval cities were well supplied with hospitals, most of them run by religious orders. But medicine was still in such a primitive state that little could be done except to keep the patients as comfortable as possible and away from healthy people who might otherwise become infected. When the Black Death ravaged Europe in the mid-1300s, one could only bury the dead. This terrible plague killed perhaps one third of the people in Europe.

For the survivors of the Black Death, there was the business of living to get on with. In busy towns such as Bruges, the merchants continued their trading and became even more prosperous. In the 1400s, as we have seen, the city was at the peak of its brilliance. But, very quietly, nature was undermining the prosperity of the Flemish port. Its harbor and channel were clogging up with silt. By the end of the century, on a typical day, only 33 ships arrived in the harbor— compared to 100 or more a day in earlier years. The city government did what it could by way of dredging, but it was no match for nature. The merchants of Europe found new markets, such as nearby Antwerp. The English began weaving their woolen cloth instead of exporting raw wool. Bruges had had its day. But other European cities were in their ascendant, and urban civilization in Europe had come to stay.

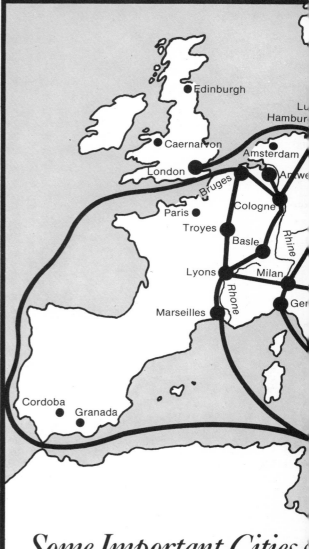

Some Important Cities
Trade Routes of the Midd

Below: Some of the most important trade routes of the Middle Ages. The map also shows the location of some of the important cities mentioned in this chapter. Notice the two main routes to the Orient: overland through central Asia and by sail through the Red Sea. By the time ships like these 16th-century Dutch merchant vessels (left) were sailing out, many new trade routes had been discovered.

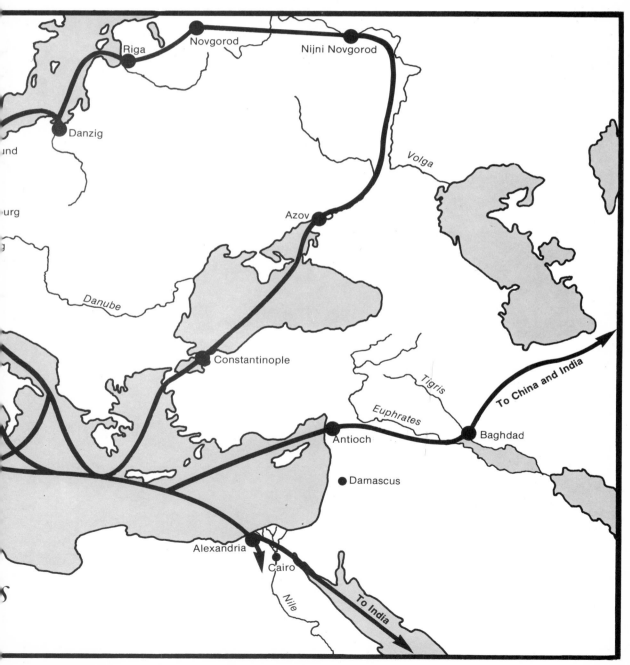

The Grand Design

4

The Piazza of St. Peter in Rome. The imposing façade of the church and the great curve of the colonnades enclosing the piazza perfectly illustrate the feeling for grandeur and the lavish use of space that began to influence the planning of cities from the 1600s onward, in both Europe and the New World.

IN ST. PETER'S SQUARE, in Rome, we are in a world very different from the narrow, introspective streets of a medieval city. Clearly, a new kind of city has come into being. Splendor has re-entered the picture.

Under the caesars Rome had been a splendid city, full of triumphal ways, temples, and arenas—the capital of the western civilized world. After the fall of the empire and the raids of the barbarians, the city was in a state of decline. Apart from being the seat of the popes, medieval Rome had little distinction. Its ancient structures crumbled and were dismantled by citizens in search of building materials. In the 1500s people led their cattle to graze among the stones of the forum—which soon became known as the Campo Vaccino, or "cow field." Among the proud cities of medieval Italy, Rome ranked rather low.

But already by the 1500s some of the popes had begun to transform their city. They intended to build a city that would surpass ancient Rome in grandeur. It would be a visible assertion of the majesty of the Catholic Church—at a time, ironically, when the Church was being challenged on several sides. It was urban renewal on a grand scale.

Considering the old St. Peter's Basilica inadequate as the Mother Church of Christendom, Pope Julius II (1503-13) had it torn down and set the architect Bramante to work on a new design. Several other architects, including Michelangelo, added their genius to the project. The result, completed in 1590, is a magnificent structure, capable of holding 50,000 people. Many other churches, palaces, and public buildings were built in Rome throughout the 16th and 17th centuries.

Some popes concentrated on individual buildings, but Pope Sixtus V turned his attention to the city as a whole. Between 1585 and 1590, he and his architect Domenico Fontana conceived a master plan for the growing city. It embraced areas outside the medieval city, including some of the hills on which ancient Rome had stood. Some of these landmarks were already capped by churches. Sixtus proposed to link them with a network of avenues. "Our Lord," explained Fontana, "now wishing to ease the way for those, who, prompted by devotions or vows, are accustomed to visit frequently the most holy places of the city . . . opened many commodious and straight streets in many places. Thus one can by foot, by horse, or in a carriage start from whatever place in Rome one may wish, and continue virtually in a straight line to the most famous devotions."

The main thoroughfare in Sixtus' Rome was the Strada Felice. It was about $2\frac{1}{2}$ miles long, "straight as a plumb line and wide enough to allow five carriages to ride abreast." Other major avenues went southward from the Strada Felice to connect with short avenues that had recently been built

This imaginary city, attributed to 15th-century architect Luciano Laurana, not only displays the artist's skill in the use of perspective, but also conveys the Renaissance feeling for order and symmetry in city planning. The right-hand side of the picture (not shown) perfectly balances the buildings on the left.

in the medieval city. Sixtus further improved the city with a system of many wash houses and public fountains, a scheme unparalleled since the days of the caesars.

Many of the fountains that splash in Roman piazzas were designed by Bernini, architect of St. Peter's Square. Bernini worked for a number of popes as well as for some of the wealthy Roman families, and it was he, more than any other single artist, who gave the city its special quality of exuberant grandeur—what we call the *baroque* style in art and architecture. Bernini's work is very theatrical. His statues portray people running and leaping, horses rearing back on their hind legs, action in every line. It comes as no surprise that Bernini was a successful stage designer. His scenic effects were so startlingly realistic that Roman theatergoers were sometimes frightened out of their seats by apparent floods and fires.

The taste for the baroque that influenced the rebuilding of Rome also influenced the building of other cities. Between the end of the Middle Ages and the beginning of the Industrial Revolution—roughly 1500 to 1800—the western city achieved a grandeur that Europe had never seen before. As always, there were variations, from country to country and from one generation to the next. But throughout these 300 or so years, there was a noticeable trend toward *planning* cities (rather than just letting them grow), and of superimposing order upon older cities. The plans reflected people's love of

harmony, symmetry, and ornamentation. They also reflected a shift in the power structure in Europe.

Around the 1500s, the status of the city had begun to change. In fact, the whole pattern of western European life—economic, social, religious, intellectual, and political—was changing. Medieval cities had enjoyed varying degrees of independence. In Italy, for example, there were many city-states, entirely self-governing and having jurisdiction over the surrounding region. Many of these had republican forms of government. In northern Europe, the towns belonging to the Hanseatic League controlled trade around the Baltic Sea and formed a powerful bloc for their mutual benefit. Many Italian and German towns coined their own money. Even in parts of Europe where towns were subservient to a lord or a king (notably in France and England), they usually exerted some influence in the land. A town could force the peasants of the surrounding area to sell their produce only in the town's market and could restrict the production of man-made goods to their own craft guilds.

Where there was no nation the city commanded the patriotic sentiments of the people. There was no Italian state until 1861; no Germany until 1871. A citizen of Florence did not consider himself an Italian, but a Florentine, and was justifiably proud of the fact. That city, more than any other, produced the revival of classical learning and the great surge of artistic creativity that we call the Renaissance. Ideas that eventually affected the whole of Europe were born and nourished in Florence.

But even while Florence prospered, it was being outstripped in power by larger political units—the nations. Monarchs of England, France, Spain, and other countries were consolidating their lands and control over their subjects. Centralization was the trend of the times—a trend that was to continue into modern times and that can be seen in the United States today, in the gradual decline of states' rights. Those areas where the cities had been most independent and

The airy, graceful arches of the Library of San Marco, in Florence, convey something of the spirit of the Renaissance, which had its first flowering in this city. The glass cases hold some of the writings of ancient Greece and Rome that revolutionized European thought.

The Fountain of the Four Rivers, in the Piazza Navona, Rome, typifies the exuberance of Italian baroque sculpture and, in particular, of its creator, Bernini—who also designed the colonnade of the Piazza of St. Peter.

82

powerful, Italy and Germany, remained divided and relatively weak, while the emerging nations increasingly controlled events in Europe and extended their economic and political influence into the New World.

The growing power of the state was accompanied by a decline in the power of the Church. Once the Reformation had split Christianity into Catholic and Protestant, heads of state seized the opportunity to decide which religion their subjects should follow. One willful king, Henry VIII of England, severed relations with Rome and declared himself head of the Church in England. Even in countries that remained Catholic, the government generally gained some control over Church administration.

While the Church as an institution was being challenged by the state, some of the church's beliefs were being challenged by the new discoveries of science. Many educated men were now less inclined to accept the teachings of religion as they related to the natural world. In a word, Europe was becoming secular.

The shift from sacred to secular appeared in the new urban landscape. Where the center of a medieval city was the cathedral, the place of honor in the new city was usually the palace. The focal point of medieval Paris was the cathedral of Notre Dame, whose towers and flying buttresses direct the eye heavenward. By contrast, the focal point of Louis XIV's "new town" of Versailles was the palace. Here, the emphasis is horizontal.

83

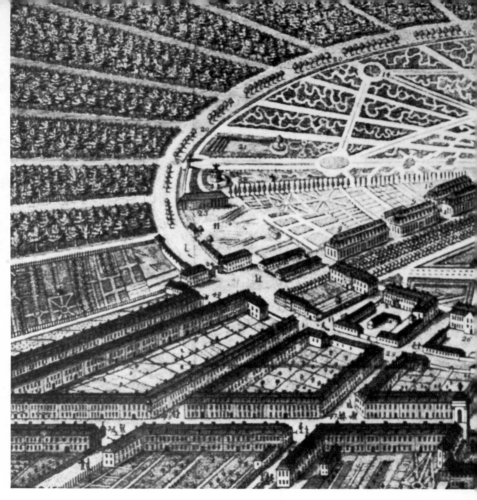

This 18th-century view of Karlsruhe, capital of Baden-Würtemburg in Germany, shows the passion for order and symmetry in the town-planning of the time, and the glorification of the prince, whose palace was the focal point of many European capitals. Louis XIV, the "Sun King," had set the style with his magnificent Palace of Versailles, and other rulers throughout Europe did their best to imitate it.

The great expanse of building and gardens, spreading over the land, proclaims worldly power—specifically the power of the state, represented by the king.

The centralization of power in the state meant that the capital city quickly surpassed the other cities of the realm in size and importance. London's population increased from an estimated 200,000 in 1600 to 675,000 in 1750, making it the largest city in Europe. Most of this growth was due to immigration from the provinces. London, Madrid, Vienna and other capitals became not only the political centers of their respective nations, but the commercial, cultural, and social centers as well. There were variations on this pattern: Paris and nearby Versailles formed a sort of joint capital city after 1682; and the government of Holland sat at The Hague, whereas the commercial and cultural life centered in Amsterdam.

Aside from the burgeoning capitals, there was little urban growth. From 1500 to 1800 the proportion of Europeans living in cities remained fairly static: between 10 and 15 per cent. (Of course, this percentage varied from one country to another.) Today, by contrast, 35 per cent of Europe's population live in cities of more than 20,000: 21 per cent in cities of more than 100,000.

Cities had grown rapidly in the early Middle Ages, partly because of an overall population growth, but mainly because they attracted people by offering safety and freedom. Gradually, these two aspects of city life lost their significance. The country-side was made safer by governments wishing to encourage long-distance trade. And the loosening of the bonds between peasant and lord meant that the peasant no longer looked to the town for his freedom.

Then, as now, "freedom" was a relative term. A French peasant of the 1700s was no

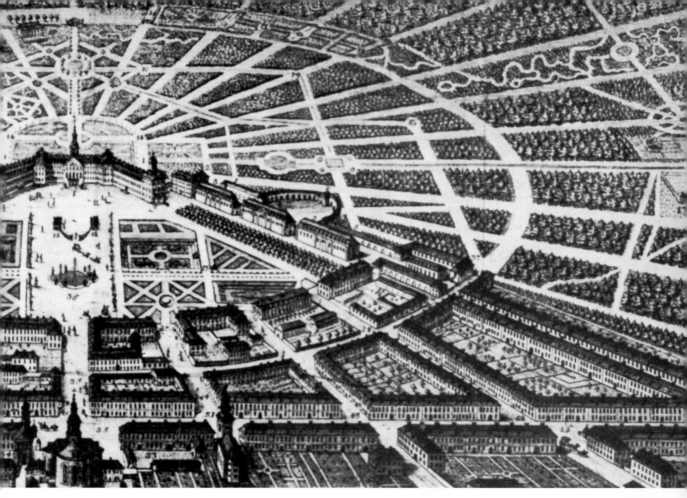

longer bound to his lord's service, as his ancestor of the 1200s had been (or as a Russian serf still was), but he bore a heavy burden of taxes imposed by the state. Powerful monarchs arbitrarily established what rights the citizens could enjoy. The same was true of the rights of towns. Louis XIV, needing more money to finance his foreign wars, annulled many towns' charters, then restored some of their civic rights for a high price.

Absolute power could accomplish a great deal—though usually at the expense of the people. Tsar Peter the Great (reigned 1672-1725) is remembered because he pulled Russia into a position of military power and opened its doors to western culture. As an absolute monarch Peter could achieve something that the representative government of the young United States later found very difficult: he built, from scratch, a new capital city, and a very magnificent one, too.

St. Petersburg (now Leningrad) is located on the Neva River, where it flows into the Gulf of Finland. The original settlement was an island fortress, which the tsar had quickly built up in 1703 to defend his newly conquered territory from recapture by the Swedes. The position was very important, because it gave Russia access to the Baltic Sea and helped to encourage trade and cultural exchange between Russia and the rest of Europe. The building of the fort required the labor of 40,000 men—many of whom died from exposure to the icy water in which they worked laying the foundations.

When Peter set about building the city itself, he hired the best architects he could find. The result was one of the most beautiful cities in Europe. It was also one of the most regimented. Peter wanted to create an extremely well-ordered and stratified society. He designated three basic house plans for the nobility, the bourgeoisie, and the lower classes. Any citizen wishing to build a house according to a design of his own choosing must have the design approved by the government. Peter also divided the city into districts for the various classes and occupations: aristocracy in one neighborhood, craftsmen in another, and so on. At frequent intervals, the citizens were summoned by the beating of a drum to gather in Troitza Square to listen to one of the many edicts issued by the tsar.

Understandably, there was not much popular enthusiasm for moving to St. Petersburg and living under the tsar's all-seeing eye. Some of the new residents refused to live in the areas appointed for them. On two occasions, Peter cracked down on these defiant subjects. He had some of them

The citizens of St. Petersburg are shown celebrating the city's 100th anniversary in 1803. In the center of the painting is a temporary bridge of boats, leading to a statue of Peter the Great and the Cathedral of St. Isaac. By this time the population of St. Petersburg had grown to over 200,000.

evicted and had the roofs torn from their newly built houses.

Few residents of European capitals experienced anything like the strict regulation suffered by Peter's subjects. But most of them were familiar to some extent with the heavy hand of the government, and in particular of the military "establishment." Most of the great capitals housed large standing armies.

In the mid-1700s Berlin, capital of the young state of Prussia, had a military population of more than 21,000, almost a quarter of the total population of the city.

During the Renaissance, fortification had become an elaborate and costly affair. Earlier, in the Middle Ages, a city's defenses had been relatively simple, consisting of a wall and a few towers. But when, in the 1300s, armies began to use weapons fired with gunpowder, these defenses proved inadequate. Military engineers set to work designing stronger and stronger fortifications. Usually these consisted of several rows of ramparts with projecting points, or *bastions*, where the defenders could fire at the attackers before the latter got within firing distance of the city itself.

The main drawback to these defenses—besides their enormous expense—was that they tended to stifle a city's growth. The medieval wall could be knocked down and rebuilt farther out with relatively little expense. But the massive earthworks and masonry of the Renaissance were virtually immovable. Overcrowding became a problem for many of these encased cities. Eventually, the defenses became more trouble than they were worth, and many were destroyed.

The design of the fortifications reflected the new passion for order and symmetry. In the 1600s, scientists such as Galileo, Kepler, and Newton, as they uncovered what seemed to be a most orderly universe, formulated scientific laws. Architects and city planners tried to impose a similar order on their environment. The "surprise" element, so strong in the medieval town, gave way to the formal pattern.

Left: This view of Vienna in 1683 shows the elaborate fortifications that persisted throughout the Renaissance and later. The overcrowded population spilled out to form suburbs around the walls. Below: A map of 17th-century Amsterdam, with its concentric plan of interconnecting canals.

The chief element in most of these plans was the avenue. For the planner with military considerations in mind, it had a strategic value. It was difficult to move troops through narrow medieval streets while maintaining formation. So the planners allowed for wide, straight streets, so that troops defending a city could get rapidly from Point A to Point B, when and if the fortifications at Point B were penetrated by the enemy.

The usefulness of wide avenues in controlling the city's own inhabitants was appreciated many years later by the French planner Baron Haussmann. He was the man responsible for Paris being, of all the cities in the world, the best endowed with grand boulevards. They cut across the city, intersecting each other at oblique angles and giving an impressive "sweep" to the Parisian landscape. Many, such as the famous Champs Elysées, are lined with trees and sidewalk cafés. But beautiful vistas were only a secondary consideration with Haussmann when, in the 1850s, he began to rebuild parts of Paris. He stressed to the city council that wide avenues would afford "a simplified defense on days of riots." The Parisian mob had effectively barricaded many of the narrow streets during the revolution of 1848, and a smaller uprising in 1852 had further demonstrated to Haussmann and to his employer, the Emperor Napoleon III, the importance of some anti-riot measures. Broad avenues, cutting through the rabbit warren of old Parisian streets, would do the job. In the event of a popular uprising, troops could move swiftly through the city, isolate small groups of rioters, and so keep the populace from joining forces.

89

The avenue *par excellence*. The long straight sweep of the Champs Elysées, flowing down from the Arc de Triomphe, perfectly expresses the French feeling for "gloire" and national pride. Freed of its frenetic motor traffic, the avenue here serves as an appropriate setting for a Bastille Day parade, including cadets from the academy of Saint-Cyr. The academy's most illustrious alumnus, Napoleon Bonaparte, commissioned the building of the massive Arch to commemorate some of the great French victories.

It was not so much the army as carriage-borne traffic that really created the need for the avenue. Traffic in medieval times had consisted mainly of pedestrians, plus an occasional rider on horseback. Under these conditions, narrow, unpaved streets caused no great problems. But when more and more people began riding in carriages, these narrow streets were inadequate. The traffic jam was born.

Straight, broad avenues not only provided a practical solution to the congestion, but also allowed drivers to show off the speed of their horses—and to suggest the importance of the owner. Horsepower became part of the pageant of the city.

Meanwhile, the less important players in the pageant—the poor—remained pedestrians, a status that now became very disagreeable. One had to keep a sharp eye open for rushing wheels and horses' hooves, while at the same time watching where one stepped. Crossing the street required expert coordination. With no sidewalks, the poor pedestrian was literally in the gutter. Late in the 1700s sidewalks were installed in the more prosperous areas of London. A German visiting London in 1786 found them most impressive: "Wide side stones, or rather slabs, have been placed along both sides of the streets, so that the pedestrians can walk in safety and comfort in the most populated areas, even in the greatest confusion of carriages. No coachman may touch these side stones under fine of 20 shillings."

Those who couldn't afford to maintain a carriage, horses, and driver, might hire a cab on occasion. Then, as now, the operation had its difficulties. The French writer Louis Sebastian Mercier describes a scene in Paris in the 1780s:

"At two o'clock those who have invitations to dine set out, dressed in their best, powdered, adjusted, and walking on tiptoe not to soil their stockings. All the cabs are engaged, not one is to be found on the rank; there is a good deal of competition for these vehicles, and you may see two would-be fares carry a cab by assault from different sides, jumping in together and furiously disputing which was first; on which the cabman whips up and drives them both off to the Commissary of Police, who takes the burden of decision off his shoulders."

All of which goes to show that certain aspects of city life never really change.

Today, the avenue continues to be an important element in city planning. Even aside from the hotly debated issue of traffic requirements *versus* the pedestrian, the wide street has a symbolic appeal for many planners. In Brazil's new capital of Brasilia, where space is abundant and traffic still relatively sparse, the main ceremonial avenue is 680 feet wide. The baroque spirit is still alive.

Ostentatious wealth was one of the features distinguishing the baroque from the medieval city; severe poverty was another. There had been rich and poor in the Middle Ages, but nothing like the extremes of wealth and want that developed in the 1500s and 1600s. Great fortunes began to be made by a few enterprising—and lucky—individuals, while the great mass of the people, less enterprising perhaps, and certainly less lucky, found themselves at the bottom of the ladder, without much chance of climbing upward. In between, the people of the growing middle class lived in modest comfort and tried to better their fortunes.

Over a period of several hundred years, beginning in the later Middle Ages, western Europe experienced a commercial revolution. As with most revolutions, its causes, characteristics, and effects were many and complex. Centralization was one of its aspects. In medieval Europe, industry and trade had been primarily local. A town would contain, say, 25 weavers, including masters, journeymen, and apprentices, who made cloth for the citizens of that town and for the peasants of the surrounding area. The typical master weaver was his own merchant as well. But when long-distance trade began to develop, a distinct class of

Above. A fashionable conveyance in 18th-century London was the sedan chair. In this print, entitled *The Last Bit of Scandal*, two elegant acquaintances stop to exchange gossip, while their bearers (one of whom seems to be yawning) hold up the roofs.

Left: The Royal Exchange, financial nerve center of Britain, pictured in 1788. Britain's growing overseas empire gave her great economic power, and the transactions in this building in London helped to make possible the growth of the industrial towns described in the following chapter.

merchants came into being. At first, they were itinerant, moving from one fair to the next. Then, as they made more money, many of them were able to establish headquarters and expand their operations. They could hire agents and send them to the various trading centers. The agents would take large orders for the commodity the merchant was dealing in—say, cloth. The merchant would fill the orders by employing a great number of weavers. Many of these craftsmen were country people, working in their own homes. This "putting-out" system became the normal method of production in Europe until the Industrial Revolution. There were, however, a few prototype factories in Europe long before the machine age. In 1540 John Winchcombe of Newbury, England, owned 200 looms and employed 600 men, women, and children in his establishment.

Large-scale business operations demanded large amounts of capital for their financing. The successful became more successful. Overseas trade offered a chance to make a fortune, to those merchants who had enough resources to risk some of them on a venture

93

that might end in shipwreck or an attack by pirates. Investing was encouraged by the establishment of stock exchanges. The importance of this institution is suggested by the fact that the focal point of Sir Christopher Wren's plan for the rebuilding of London after the Great Fire of 1666 was not St. Paul's Cathedral (designed by Wren himself) but the Royal Exchange. Wren's plan was never carried out, but its implication that money transactions are the heart of a city reflected the new thinking of his day.

People who had money to invest began to make huge profits. Europe's wealthy financiers loaned money to heads of state and thus became very powerful. They married into the nobility, and some were made nobles themselves.

The nobility were often glad enough to marry their sons and daughters to the newly rich bourgeoisie (even though money from "trade" was considered not quite respectable), for many of their own fortunes had now shrunk drastically. Severe inflation had hit Europe in the mid-1500s. The great influx of gold from the Americas meant more money in circulation, and hence higher prices. Between 1500 and 1650, the price of wheat and hay in the Paris market increased 15 times over. Landed gentry, whose incomes came from fixed rents paid by tenant farmers, found they could not keep up with rising prices. Many were forced to sell their estates to rich merchants who wanted to live in aristocratic style.

At the other end of the social scale, the wage-earners were also caught in the wage-price squeeze. Their earnings rarely kept pace with the increase in prices. The poor formed a very large part of urban populations. Their dissatisfaction occasionally erupted, as in the many riots of late 18th-century London, and, more spectacularly, in the French Revolution, when the Paris mob released rage that had been smoldering for generations.

Prosperity was more widespread in the strongly bourgeois society of the Dutch Republic. This country became, in the early 1600s, a great commercial power. Its largest city, Amsterdam, was—along with London—the major banking center of Europe and also the main port of Europe's largest navy (until surpassed by the English). The city's affluence had first come as an indirect result of a decline in the herring population of the Baltic Sea. The Hanseatic League towns no longer controlled this fishing industry; and the people of Amsterdam fished more intensively for the North Sea herring and soon controlled the European market. According to an old saying, "Amsterdam was built on herring bones."

Between 1567 and 1630, Amsterdam's population increased from 30,000 to 115,000. Many foreigners were attracted to the city, partly because of its commercial opportunities, and partly because of the religious toleration practiced by the Dutch government. Thousands of French Protestants and Spanish and Portuguese Jews made new homes in Amsterdam and contributed to the city's prosperity.

Fortunately, the rapid growth of the city was accomplished by a comprehensive plan for its development. The Amsterdam Council authorized the digging of new canals and the

preparation of new land for building; they ordered the zoning of the city into industrial and residential areas; and they specified the maximum area of a lot that could be devoted to construction.

Building in Amsterdam was difficult. The sandy soil sometimes required foundations to be sunk 60 feet. But the difficulty of the task did not daunt the people of Amsterdam. Thanks to their energy, farsightedness, and abundant wealth, the city grew quickly and harmoniously. Even today, Amsterdam has a remarkably unified appearance. Its many canals, lined with graceful trees and tall brick 17th- and 18th-century houses, help to make it one of Europe's most charming cities.

Much of what we know about the people of Amsterdam and other Dutch towns comes from the work of Dutch painters. Affluent citizens wanted pictures to decorate their comfortable homes. The existence of a good market for paintings attracted artists to the cities, particularly to Amsterdam. Painters of the Dutch School painted scenes of rural and urban life and portraits of their bourgeois patrons. In the monarchies, artists also gravitated to the capitals, where they painted the royal and noble families. The fine arts were less and less under the patronage of the Church, and more and more under the patronage of secular society, whether bourgeois or aristocratic.

The theater, which in medieval times has taken the form of mystery and miracle plays, now began to go its own way independently of the Church, and it became a very popular form of entertainment. On London's South Bank in the 1500s and 1600s, the Globe and several other theaters offered comedy, tragedy, and historical drama to audiences drawn from all levels of society. Traveling players took the theater to the provinces, but it was in the major cities—as it still is today—that the art really flourished. It was for the London audience that Marlowe, Jonson, and Shakespeare wrote.

Somewhat later, operas and concerts also began to attract large audiences. Although

Below: A city plan that remained only a plan. After the Great Fire of 1666 destroyed most of the old City of London, the architect Christopher Wren submitted a plan for the rebuilding of the city. A prominent feature of the design is the system of diagonal avenues superimposed on a modified grid pattern. The main focal point of the new City would be the Royal Exchange (to right of center). The plan was not used, and the streets of the City remain irregular and curving, intersecting at odd angles.

still dependent on royal patronage to a great extent, composers and performers found increasing demand among the public for good music.

In general, it was the very large cities that offered the best talent. But even capitals of small duchies and principalities often enjoyed a stimulating cultural life. When we

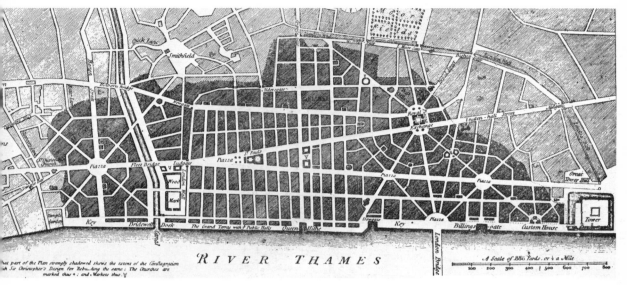

RIVER THAMES

Edinburgh well illustrates some of the differences between medieval and 18th-century town planning. Above left: A typical street in the Old Town with its tall houses pressed close together. Left: The spacious and orderly New Town, with wide sidewalks and gaslight (circa 1840).

look at a tiny but lively German capital, such as Weimar, we are reminded that the essential quality of being a city may have little to do with size.

The population of Weimar, capital of a small Saxon duchy, was less than 6,000 when the poet Johann Wolfgang von Goethe went to live there in 1775. According to the French writer Mme. de Staël, it was "not so much a small town as a large château." A third of the area within its walls was taken up by the duke's establishment. The remaining area contained some 600 or 700 houses (some of them mere cottages), a few shops, a town hall, a church, and a marketplace. Cattle owned by the citizens were driven through the cobbled streets out to pasture.

Weimar was technically a "city" by virtue of being the capital and the residence of the duke. But its real claim to city status was the brilliance of its intellectual life, which was stimulated not only by Goethe but also by the playwright Schiller and the

philosopher Herder. The prestige of the Weimar court was recognized throughout Europe, and the work of its most illustrious minds had far-reaching influence.

In contrast to Weimar, the palace of Versailles might have been described as "not so much a large château as a small city." For many years it was the virtual capital of France. Through its miles of corridors walked ministers and lesser bureaucrats intent on business of state, courtiers intriguing for positions of power, and an army of servants making the whole establishment function. Sedan chairs could be hired by those too lazy to walk. The public were admitted to the palace with little supervision; the 18th-century tourist could wander freely through most of its rooms. It is estimated that the palace could house 10,000 people. In its lavish way, it was the forerunner of some modern plans for cities, in which entire communities would live and work in one giant building.

Many of the courtiers at Versailles lived

Left: This view of the royal stables seen from the king's bedchamber, painted by Jean-Baptiste Martin, about 1690, depicts some of the color and pageantry of life at Versailles under the Sun King. In the foreground some courtiers organize a hunting party. Others ride off on business or pleasure in coaches and sedan chairs. In the background, soldiers are drilling. (Louis XIV was continually at war.) The symmetry of the buildings and the lavish use of space is typical of baroque architecture.

in rather cramped quarters in the farther reaches of the palace, and exhausted their small fortunes trying to keep up with the expensive court life. The great nobles spent most of the day hovering around the king—performing elaborate rituals such as those attending his getting dressed in the morning and getting undressed at night. Especially in the reign of Louis XIV, the "Sun King," life at Versailles meant continual devotion to a personality cult. Everyone would stand around in anticipation waiting for the king to pass through on his way to Mass or to dinner, hoping for a nod, a smile, a look. If one wasn't looked at for several days, it was taken as a sign of royal disfavor. All the same, one had better be present; absence without

Right: Although entitled *An Architectural Caprice,* this painting by Guardi was obviously inspired by the streets, squares, and arcades of 18th-century Venice. Once a powerful republic and one of the major trading centers of Europe, and later the home of a great school of painting, Venice was now in decline. In the canvases of Guardi and Canaletto the city is revealed as a city devoted to spectacle.

leave from the king was social suicide. It was Louis's policy to keep the nobility near him, so that he could keep an eye on them. For his part, he did his best to keep them entertained. Hunts, masquerades, lavish theatrical spectacles, followed each other with hardly a pause. But perhaps the main attraction of life at Versailles was simply the exhilarating sense of being at the center of power.

By the 1700s, London had become the largest city in Europe, and one of the most stimulating. "A man who is tired of London," said Dr. Johnson, "is tired of life." The city was elegant and sordid, cultivated and cruel, frivolous and intellectual, both green and spacious and crowded and dirty. Johnson's own London centered around the City—that is, the original City of London before the capital embraced the surrounding villages of Mayfair, Bloomsbury, Chelsea, and others. The City was—and is—the financial center of Britain. It is also the legal center and, since the 1700s, the center of journalism. Dozens of weeklies and some daily newspapers made their appearance in the 1700s and were edited and printed in the area around Fleet Street. (Today "Fleet Street" stands for British journalism, just as "Wall Street" stands for American finance.)

Many of the newspapers were "born" in the various London coffeehouses. These were very popular establishments in the 18th century.

A man would go to his favorite coffeehouse to hear the latest gossip, read the newspapers, arrange a business deal, or play a game of cards with his friends. Each coffeehouse had its regular clientele. For example, the Bedford coffeehouse in Covent Garden was host to a number of literary men, including the poet Alexander Pope, the novelist (and magistrate) Henry Fielding, and the playwright Richard Brinsley Sheridan. The celebrated actor David Garrick might drop in before a performance of Sheridan's *School for Scandal* at the nearby Covent Garden Theatre. There were pubs, too (called taverns in those days), which served wines and spirits and meals. At the "Crown and Anchor" Dr. Johnson held forth to his friend Boswell and to anyone else who would listen, expounding opinions on every subject.

Unlike some other European capitals, London was not, as a whole, planned; it accumulated. Some individual areas were laid out in rectangular blocks after the 1600s, but there was (and is) no "grand design" overlying the whole city. Gradually the parts grew together, each retaining to some extent its original character. The city of Westminster, seat of the court and parliament, attracted the rich and fashionable people. In their wake followed merchants, tailors, cabinetmakers, and other craftsmen, who supplied them with the luxury goods they required. Many of the elegant shops of present-day Mayfair were first established in the 1700s.

It was about this time that shopping became a form of entertainment. Buying had been a necessary and regular activity of the

The London of the coffeehouses (right) where the middle and upper classes could enjoy good conversation in pleasant surroundings coexisted with the London of unspeakable squalor—at left, *Gin Lane* by William Hogarth—where poor Londoners lived.

medieval town. The weekly market and the craft shops had supplied the citizens with the goods they needed to maintain their simple households. Now, the vast quantity and variety of goods on display attracted great crowds of shoppers, who would spend the whole day buying, window-shopping, and discussing their purchases or just chatting with the friends they encountered:

"I have heard that some ladies... have taken their coaches and spent a whole afternoon in Ludgate Street or Covent Garden, only to divert themselves in going from one mercer's shop to another, to look upon their fine silks and to rattle and banter the shopkeepers, having not so much as the least occasion, much less intention, to buy anything."

The introduction of plate glass in the 1700s gave shopkeepers new opportunities to display their wares. A German visitor to London in 1775 was amazed by their mercantile extravagance:

"On the street floors there are shops that seem to be built completely of glass; thousands of lights illuminate silverware shops; stores with engravings on display, book stores; stores where one may see watches, glass, pewter, ladies' dresses and finery. . . . The confectioners' displays blind one's eyes . . . with their brilliant candelabras."

The color, grandeur, and pomp of the avenues were supported by armies of people who served the richer classes, either directly as domestic servants, or indirectly, laboring in factories or shipyards, or even in the workhouses provided by the city to occupy the unemployed, working from 6 A.M. till 8 P.M. Domestic servants were at least adequately fed and clothed, and many of them lived in good neighborhoods in modest houses behind the mansions of the rich. Less fortunate workers lived in the growing slum areas of the city, in miserable tenements full of disease, crime, and vice.

In the mid-1700s, a silk-weaver, for example, might earn 12 shillings a week. Lodgings in a tenement for himself and his family might cost only one or two shillings, but bread—the major item in a poor family's diet—could cost as much as five shillings a week, leaving about five shillings for all other expenses: clothing, an occasional bit of meat, a tankard of ale. If he got into debt, he would be thrown into a debtors' prison and remain there until someone paid his creditors. If he became ill, he could go to one

of the city's hospitals, where he would occupy a bug-infested bed and be cared for by an untrained nurse. If his disease was judged incurable, he would probably be turned away (although a few hospitals for people with incurable diseases were established late in the century).

To escape temporarily from their bleak lives, the London poor took to drink. Gin, in the early 1700s, was amazingly cheap: for a penny, one could drink oneself into a stupor. Gin shops proliferated throughout the city. People even gave gin to their children, partly because milk and water were scarce and unsafe, and partly, no doubt, just to keep the children quiet. Exactly how many children died from over-consumption of gin and other spirits is not known, but a report to the House of Commons in 1751 put the figures at 9,324 children each year. Parliament passed several acts against the distillation, importation, and sale of gin, and eventually succeeded in sharply cutting down its consumption. People began drinking beer and ale instead of gin.

As an alternative to the drunken stupor, there was the thrill of violence. Among the most popular entertainments in 18th-century London were bear-baiting, bull-baiting, dog-fights, and wrestling matches—including bouts between women. There was the perennial attraction of Charing Cross, where

Open space is an important part of any city plan. It provides the necessary distance for admiring beautiful buildings and a break in the sequence of streets, one after another. The green of London's Bedford Square (above) perfectly complements the dignity of the surrounding Georgian terrace houses (now mainly offices).

102

Left: The Piazza del Campo in Siena, scene of the annual *palio*, a horse-race in medieval costume.
Above: Moscow's Red Square, where Russians pay homage at the tomb of Lenin. Squares can serve as meeting places, such as this one in Salzburg, top right.

malefactors locked in the pillory offered an irresistible target for raw eggs and rotten vegetables. And on eight days a year one could enjoy "Tyburn Fair"—the public hangings that were the penalty for many trivial offenses. Every window between Newgate Prison and Tyburn Hill was filled with people cheering and jeering the victims as they passed by on their way to the gallows.

It was not only the lower classes who patronized such amusements. Members of the middle class and the aristocracy had equally callous and brutal tastes. For a while, it was the fashion on Sunday afternoons to visit the mental hospital of Bedlam to laugh at the antics of the unfortunate inmates who were exhibited like wild beasts.

But most of the amusements of London society, rich and poor, were more frivolous than brutal. They gambled and drank—the difference being that the rich gambled for high stakes and drank the best brandy. They masqueraded and flirted at Vauxhall, Ranelagh, and other pleasure gardens. They shopped and gossiped.

For all its frivolity and callousness, the London of the 1700s had its civilized aspects. We can see this in its architecture. Much of the charm of present-day London is an inheritance from the 18th-century builders. Perhaps their greatest contribution is the many beautiful squares—particularly those in the West End.

The square has a great variety of forms and functions. It can enclose a crowd, provide a setting for a great building, help to create a sense of community. One writer on city planning calls it "a psychological parking place within the civic landscape."

The domestic square—the kind surrounded by houses—is found on the Continent as well as in England, but the English variety is the most inviting because of its greenery. The informal planting of trees has helped to reduce the scale of the surrounding buildings and to create a truly domestic environment. These patches of green refresh the spirit and remind us that a city is most inviting when it includes some of the attractions of nature.

103

To savor fully the spirit of 18th-century urban life, one should go to Bath. This small city, located in one of the loveliest valleys of the West Country, was, after London, the most fashionable town in England. It had been a spa since Roman days (the original Roman baths were excavated early in the 1900s), and 18th-century society found "taking the waters" for real and supposed ailments a pleasant excuse for renting a house in Bath and partaking of the social life, with all its scandal and intrigue.

The scene is described well in Tobias Smollett's novel *Humphry Clinker*:

"Bath is . . . all gaiety, good humour and diversion. The eye is continually entertained with the splendour of dress and equipage . . . the merry bells ring round from morn till night. We have music in the Pump Room every morning, cotillons every forenoon in the rooms, balls twice a week, and concerts every other night, besides private assemblies and parties without number. . . . Bath . . . to be sure, is an earthly paradise. . . . Here we have ministers of state, judges, generals, bishops, projectors, philosophers, wits, poets, players, chemists, fiddlers, and buffoons. . . . This is what my uncle reprobates as a monstrous jumble of heterogeneous principles; a vile mob of noise and impertinence, without decency or subordination. But this chaos is a source of infinite amusement."

The city of Bath, shown (top) in an 18th-century watercolor by Thomas Loggoh. Above: A scene outside the Pump Room, in 1823. Invalids and elderly people could make their way to the baths by means of a "Bath chair" such as the one shown here. Much of 18th- and 19th-century Bath is now falling victim to commercial interests, but architectural gems such as the Royal Crescent (left) remain.

The glitter of Bath has gone. Fashionable society now goes to the Côte d'Azur and St. Moritz. But the elegant buildings remain—row after row of mellow golden stone façades and tall windows. A narrow street opens into the great sweep of the Royal Crescent, a terrace of nearly identical houses that form one splendid architectural whole. The plan of the city is open and flowing and well-laced with green.

The urban forms of the Old World were repeated in the New. The Spaniards built great baroque cathedrals on spacious plazas. Small New England towns have their village greens lined with comfortable frame houses. And when the leaders of the new United States of America began to build their capital city on the banks of the Potomac, they naturally turned to the cities of Europe for inspiration.

The plan for the new city was entrusted to a French military engineer named Pierre Charles L'Enfant. L'Enfant was, of course, familiar with Versailles and other examples of European city planning. In 1791, while working on the plan for the new city, he wrote to Thomas Jefferson, then in France, asking him to send plans of some of the great European cities, such as Paris, Amsterdam, Venice, and Madrid. Jefferson sent plans, adding, "I would prefer the adoption of one of the modes of antiquity" (meaning a grid, such as in Philadelphia). L'Enfant's plan was basically such a grid, but overlaid with a truly baroque system of avenues. One of these, Pennsylvania Avenue, links the executive and legislative branches of the government: the White House and the Capitol. The

105

original plan also provided for another avenue running from the Capitol to a "judiciary square" where the Supreme Court would be placed. The main avenues, one for each of the 13 colonies, tied together the separate parts of the city. They were made 160 feet wide for ease of movement (many years before today's rush-hour traffic could even be imagined). An enormous stretch of grass, the Mall, ran from the Capitol to the river. (One little-known fact about the planning of the capital is that the site was surveyed and the city plan drawn up in detail by a black farmer and astronomer—Benjamin Banneker.)

Throughout most of the 1800s, Washington's projected grandeur was unrealized. "A city of magnificent distances" was about the kindest description anyone could muster. Charles Dickens preferred to call it "the City of Magnificent Intentions." He commented on its "spacious avenues, that begin in nothing and lead nowhere; streets, mile-long, that only want houses . . . and inhabitants; public buildings that need but a public to be complete."

As Washington slowly grew, L'Enfant's plan underwent many alterations and encroachments on the part of private developers. At one point, a railroad line cut right across the Mall. In recent years, parts of the original plan have been restored, and Washington has achieved a measure of elegance. Perhaps the most handsome of its avenues is Massachusetts Avenue, which is lined with embassies and their private gardens. The art historian Kenneth Clark calls Washington "the most grandiose piece of town planning since Sixtus V's Rome."

The elegant and fashionable neighborhood of Georgetown, in Washington, is a lovely legacy from the 18th century. Below, left: A garden party at a Georgetown home. Below: A typical house on a tree-shaded street. Washington is a very green and spacious city.

But, like most cities, Washington has its seamy side with its decrepit slums and crime-infested streets. Violence is a part of 20th-century Washington, just as it was part of 18th-century London and Paris. And the existence in Washington of squalor and elegance side by side is a sobering reminder that the grand design is no solution to a city's basic ills.

Machine City

5

"IT WAS A TOWN of red brick, or of brick that would have been red if the smoke and ashes had allowed it. . . . It was a town of machinery and tall chimneys, out of which interminable serpents of smoke trailed themselves for ever and ever, and never got uncoiled. It had a black canal in it, and a river that ran purple with ill-smelling dye, and vast piles of buildings full of windows where there was a rattling and trembling all day long, and

A town built by industry and dominated by it: Leeds, in Yorkshire, shown in an engraving made in 1885. The forest of smoking chimneys represents the city's thriving wool-making industry.

where the piston of the steam-engine worked monotonously up and down, like the head of an elephant in a state of melancholy madness. It contained several large streets all very like one another, and many small streets still more like one another, inhabited by people equally like one another, who all went in and out at the same hours, with the same sound upon the same pavements, to do the same work, and to whom every day was the same as yesterday and tomorrow, and every year the counterpart of the last and the next."

Dickens was describing (in his novel *Hard Times*) the sort of city that emerged in Britain in the early 1800s. He called it

"Coketown." Some of its real names were "Manchester," "Leeds," and "Birmingham." As other countries became industrialized, they built their own "Coketowns": Essen, Lille, Pittsburgh, Chicago—cities produced by the Industrial Revolution.

Some aspects of life in the industrial city have changed considerably since Dickens wrote. Working conditions and wages have improved, and, although pockets of squalor exist even now, the widespread poverty of the 1800s has disappeared. But the industrial city itself remains. It is a fact of 20th-century life. The physical realities of the industrial city affect not only the people who live in it, but also the people and animals, the air and the water for many miles around.

The baroque city had its share of squalor. But as a whole it was orderly, spacious, and beautiful. Its architects, builders, and planners obviously thought of a city as a desirable place to live. Some writers had weighed the relative merits of town and country, but few had suggested that the city was degrading, ugly, and evil.

By the mid-1800s, however, many people thought of the city this way. It was not only the new industrial cities that inspired loathing, but also those cities that had some claim to beauty and distinction. The art critic John Ruskin described London as "that great foul city of London—rattling, growling, smoking, stinking—a ghastly heap of fermenting brickwork, pouring out poison at every pore." In the United States, which had no strong urban tradition, the growth of cities was viewed with regret by many people. Thomas Jefferson called cities "ulcers on the body politic." He regarded the "mobs" of the great cities as a potential threat to good government, and felt that the urban environment destroyed "the manners and spirit" of the people. Later in the century, when American cities were growing by leaps and bounds, the distrust of the city grew also. Books warned young people of its dangers. A popular title of 1873 was *Tricks, Traps, and Pitfalls of City Life*.

Whatever "pitfalls" the industrial city may have offered, it certainly offered work.

The faces of these coal miners reflect the grim and hazardous nature of their job, helping to support an industrialized nation. They have better wages than their 19th-century predecessors, but they live in surroundings very similar to those of 100 years ago.

Right: A cheerier view of the industrial town is conveyed in the work of L.S. Lowry, who focused on the human aspect—while not ignoring the smokestacks.

For an enterprising man with a little capital it offered the chance to make a fortune. For a laboring man it offered merely a place beside a machine.

The Industrial Revolution, which was to create the unsightly industrial city, got underway in England in the late 1700s. Wealthy English landowners had been acquiring more and more land, until most of England's arable land was owned by relatively few people. These great landlords also had the capital necessary to invest in new methods of agriculture, and many of the experiments they tried proved highly successful. Scientific selection worked miracles in animal breeding. The average weight of cattle at London's Smithfield Market in 1710 was 370 pounds; in 1795 it was 800 pounds. Sheep improved from 18 to 80 pounds. Rotation of crops resulted in more food from the same land.

The new efficiency in food production meant that fewer people were needed on the land. In 1770 the agricultural population of Britain was 42 per cent; by 1841 it had declined to 22 per cent. The large class of people who no longer had any rural occupation flocked to the towns and cities, where the jobs were.

The population of Europe had been steadily increasing since the mid-1600s. In 1750 it was 140 million; by 1850 it had reached 266 million. But the urban population rose even more sharply than the population as a whole. In Britain in 1801 there were still only 15 towns with more than 20,000 people; by 1851 the number had increased to 63; and by 1891, to 185. London reached the million mark by 1811 and was over 4 million by 1891. Paris doubled its population between 1851 and 1891.

The growth of such long-established cities was impressive enough. But the really dramatic spectacle of the 1800s was the mushrooming growth of cities created by the new industry. In 1829, Middlesbrough, in northern England, was a hamlet of 40 people; by 1841 its population was 5,463, and by 1900—now a thriving center of iron

and coal production—it had topped 100,000. Manchester, established in the late 1700s as the center of the new cotton-manufacturing industry, numbered 70,000 inhabitants in its first census in 1801. Thirty years later, it had more than doubled, reaching 142,000. The USA—whose biggest city in 1800 was Philadelphia with 70,000 people—had, by 1900, 12 cities with populations over 200,000. In a single decade—1880 to 1890—Chicago had roughly doubled in size.

The picture of the 19th century that emerges clearly is of people concentrating more and more in cities, of new cities rising up overnight, and of a new urban landscape, marked by factories and machines.

Before the invention of the steam engine, manufacturing power was supplied by men, animals, wind, and water. Thus, industry could be scattered wherever man wanted it. Small flour mills could be located where there was enough water flowing to turn a mill wheel. Cloth was produced all over the country, by individual weavers operating hand looms.

The quality of goods that could be produced by such methods was relatively small. And in the early 1800s England found herself with a growing empire, growing markets, and a chance to make enormous profits—if she could deliver the goods. The great landowners, whose successful farming methods brought them more and more wealth, began to invest in the development of industry. Inventors designed machines that could increase the volume of production. The steam engine, which had undergone a series of improvements throughout the 1700s, began to be used in cotton mills in the 1780s. It was also used to pump water out of deep coal shafts—an important development, as more and more coal was needed as a fuel to run the engines themselves. Steam powered the new "railways," first used to carry coal out of the mines—later, to carry goods and passengers.

Iron was needed for the machines, and for the trains, bridges, and tunnels that soon became part of the English landscape. In 1790 Britain produced 68,000 tons of pig iron; in 1840, 400,000 tons; in 1860, 3,827,000 tons.

The new industrial towns grew up around the iron foundries and coal mines, and along the railroads. Formerly, cities had grown because they were centers of government, religion, defense, or trade. The new cities were centers of production. Many were, at first, simply a collection of factories. But to these factories people flocked in search of work and these workers needed houses. The more who came, the more houses were built—though seldom enough to keep up with the influx of people.

The factories excited a great deal of admiration. They were a totally new sight—probably as novel and dramatic to our ancestors as the Cape Canaveral launching site is to us. They were symbols of progress. A woolen mill built by the industrialist Titus Salt outside the town of Bradford in 1853 had impressive proportions for those days: it was 550 feet long and 90 feet high, with a chimney that rose 250 feet into the air. Such chimneys, belching pollutants into the air, had come to stay. At the opening of the Middlesbrough Town Hall in 1887, the mayor—replying to the Prince of Wales, who said that he had expected to find Middlesbrough "a smoky town"—expressed these sentiments: ". . . if there is one thing more than another that Middlesbrough can be said to be proud of, it is the smoke (cheers and laughter). The smoke is an indication of plenty of work (applause)—an indication of prosperous times (cheers)—an indication that . . . workpeople are being employed. . . ."

More sensitive spirits viewed factories and foundries with distaste. The Scottish poet Robert Burns scratched this verse on the window of the Carron Iron Works:

> We cam na here to view your warks,
> In hopes to be mair wise,
> But only, lest we gang to Hell,
> It may be nae surprise.

Hellish noise was another aspect of the new urban scene. One writer, describing Birmingham in the mid-1800s, observed: ". . . there is an unending clang of engines;

Left: These workers' houses in Pontlottin, Wales, are a dreary legacy of the Industrial Revolution. Many such houses still have outside toilets. The dramatic side of the Industrial Revolution is portrayed in this painting (right) of *Coalbrookdale by Night* by Philippe de Loutherbourg. Ironworks like this one, and, later, steel mills, would help to transform cities everywhere.

flame rustles, water hisses, steam roars, and from time to time, hoarse and hollow rises the thunder of the proofing house [where firearms are tested]. The people live in an atmosphere vibrating with clamour. . . ."

Today scientists are discovering some of the harmful effects that excessive noise can have upon the body. Here and there, a few efforts are being made to cut down the noise of the modern city. In the meantime, several generations of city-dwellers—particularly factory workers—have endured the brutalizing, and sometimes literally deafening, sounds of "progress."

The noise, however, was far from the most obnoxious aspect of the 19th-century industrial town. Living conditions were the great disgrace. New industrial areas that had no prior status as towns lacked the political machinery to deal with the housing shortage. Manchester did not become an incorporated town until 1838, by which time its population numbered more than 150,000.

During the first hectic decades of the 1800s any kind of shelter served the people flooding into the towns—even cellars. Existing large houses were occupied by many times the number of people for whom they had been intended. Hastily built houses had walls so thin it was a miracle they stood at all. The little space between buildings served as alleys and entryways that the sun rarely, if ever, penetrated. Land in town centers was very expensive, and in the absence of any regulations covering density of building the landlords built tenements back-to-back.

Gutter Alley, in the Belfast of the 1830s, was not unusual. It had nine two-roomed houses, which had earthen floors and ceilings that were only six feet high. In these nine houses lived 174 people—an average of nearly 10 people to each room. They had no water or sanitary facilities of any kind.

Eventually, such appalling conditions prompted authorities to establish some minimum building standards. Speculative builders regarded these as *maximum* standards. The "bye-law" houses they constructed became a standardized product. Squalor remained, but order was imposed upon it—with a vengeance. Street after street of identical, mean houses spread out from the factories in dreary regularity.

Repetition in itself was not new—or necessarily unattractive. It runs through the

elegant streets and squares of Georgian London and Bath. But here the repetition is of pleasing architectural elements—high windows, fan-lighted doors, crisp white trim. And the street plan, while orderly, has variety. The bye-law streets repeated ugliness and repeated it almost endlessly. Towns grew by an extension of featureless and mechanical rows of housing that echoed the mechanical, repetitive rhythm of the machines in the factories.

The machine dominated a worker's life. His work no longer consisted of making something with his hands; it was reduced to the tiresome task of feeding a machine. And when he went home at night, it was to streets and houses that seemed themselves to have been cut out by some great machine, undirected by any human impulse.

The grid pattern of street layout spread throughout England and the other industrialized countries. It was the most convenient way of subdividing land for sale prior to building. With some variation, the grid can be a pleasing, as well as practical, design. But applied rigidly, and repeated endlessly, with no allowance for different kinds of terrain and different functions, it becomes a bore. This is what happened to many American cities.

The English writer Rudyard Kipling, who visited Chicago in the early 1900s, described its streets this way:

"I looked down interminable vistas flanked with nine, ten, and fifteen-storied houses, and crowded with men and women, and the show impressed me with great horror. . . . There was no colour in the street and no beauty—only a maze of wire-ropes overhead and dirty stone flagging underfoot."

The railroad, which contributed so much

to the growth of industry, also contributed to the ugliness of the towns. For convenience, the stations were often put in town centers, close to the factories. Thus, the tracks naturally cut a gash through the town and in many cases transformed the city center into a wasteland of freight yards. Even some old established cities fell victim to the railroad. Edinburgh, one of the loveliest of European cities, was marred by it. To this day, railroad tracks cut through the large park in the center of town—although fortunately, on a low level so that they don't completely spoil the view of Edinburgh Castle. The new industrial city fared worse. It had neither castle, cathedral, market square, nor palace to draw the attention away from factory and railroad station.

Some of the stations, however, were rather impressive, and a few, in their way, were beautiful. The first of these was London's Euston Station (now torn down and replaced by a modern structure). Its builders celebrated the coming of the railroad by erecting a great triumphal arch with columns 45 feet high. Behind this was the station itself, a magnificent neo-Grecian hall.

The development of new engineering techniques and the discovery of steel-making methods in the mid-1800s made possible dramatic feats in architecture. St. Pancras Station, built in 1868-74, was in those days a startling achievement. Its roof is an enormous arcade of glass and steel, 690 feet long, spanning a distance of 243 feet. Even today, its soaring lightness is still one of London's impressive sights.

But the façade of the station is a quite different structure proclaiming the Victorians' love of the past. The St. Pancras Hotel is a neo-Gothic fantasy typical of its day, complete with turrets and winding stairways. The imitation Gothic structures that sprang up all over Britain, the United States, and (to a lesser extent) the Continent seem to have offered a reassuring link with the past to a generation boldly striding into the future.

There was no turning back the clock to

the medieval city. But the Victorians could, and did, embellish their towns with bits borrowed from the past. And they had their "palaces"—although these were monuments not to princely power but to industry and trade. Manchester's first Free Trade Hall, built in 1843, held 7,000 people. Soon it was considered too small, and a much larger one was built at a cost of $100,000—a lot of money in those days. The largest building in many industrial towns was the "Mechanics' Institute" or "Welfare Hall," a center of adult education and recreation. In one small North Wales mining village this hall, proudly towering over small stone cottages, is called the "Miners' Palace." The "proletariat" may have lived in poverty, but they had aspirations and a sense of identity.

The citizens of Bradford, a woolen manufacturing town, prided themselves on St. George's Hall built in 1851. It had a vast auditorium and balcony, where people could hear concerts and lectures, for it was meant to elevate the tone of society as well as to improve the town center.

Not to be outdone, the neighboring city of Leeds built a larger, more impressive hall. The Leeds Town Hall was opened in 1858 by Queen Victoria, who called it, "a lasting monument of public spirit and generous pride in the possession of municipal privileges." The people of Leeds boasted that their hall's auditorium was not only bigger than Bradford's but also bigger than the Great Hall of London's Euston Station! Civic pride was satisfied and progress publicly acknowledged.

Probably the most famous Victorian monument to progress was the Crystal Palace. It was constructed in 1851 in Hyde Park to house the Great Exhibition, in which more than 13,000 exhibitors from many countries displayed their wares. The Crystal Palace was a sort of enormous greenhouse, 1,851 feet long and 456 feet wide, having a total area of 18 acres. Live elm trees grew inside it. Another novel aspect of the building was that it was prefabricated. It was built of identical units, made elsewhere and

assembled on the site. Within nine months after the first rough sketches of the plan were submitted, the building was opened. More than six million people poured through its doors, and when the exhibition was over, the Crystal Palace was taken down and re-erected in a London suburb.

International Fairs became very popular in the 1800s. They served—as they do

Right: The Gare St.-Lazare in Paris—one of several pictures of this station painted by Claude Monet, who was fascinated by the effects of steam. A steam locomotive was (and still is) an impressive sight; and in the 1800s it symbolized power and material progress.

Left: The roof of St. Pancras Station in London. Spanning 74 feet was an achievement for a medieval architect (p. 64). With steel at his disposal, the architect of the St. Pancras train shed was able to design a roof that would span 243 feet.

today—to demonstrate the industrial and technical achievements of the participating countries. One of the most famous landmarks in the world, the Eiffel Tower, was built for the Paris Exposition of 1889. It served no purpose; it was simply a 1,000-foot-high monument to iron and skill.

Americans took to fairs with enthusiasm. The World's Columbian Exposition, held in Chicago in 1893, was visited by more than 21 million visitors, who were dazzled by the fair's splendid white classic-style buildings—and by its electric lighting.

By the 1880s, electric lighting had appeared in several cities, including Paris, London, and New York. Although gaslight lingered on in many towns because it was cheaper, bright electric lights soon began to transform city streets.

The conditions of the streets themselves remained poor until the end of the century. The early industrial towns often had no paving at all. As late as 1890, less than one third of Chicago's 2,048 miles of streets were paved, and of these about half were paved with wood blocks. Most of the eastern cities were paved with cobblestones and granite blocks, as were many European cities, including London.

Horse-drawn vehicles continued to make life difficult for the pedestrian—as well as creating business for the crossing-sweeper and the shoe-shine boy.

Probably one person in 40 in Victorian London obtained his living in the streets. Around 1850 it was estimated that there were 300 sellers of cats' meat and another 300 sellers of hot potatoes, 1,000 old-clothes men, several thousand street performers, and 30,000 push-cart venders, all crying their wares above the clatter of horses' hooves and the ring of steel tires on stone. Several thousand street performers entertained the passing crowds. There were 35,000 beggars.

Poverty on an unprecedented scale disfigured the cities of Europe and America and blighted the lives of millions of people. In London, small children went barefoot in the middle of winter. Thousands of women turned to prostitution as the only way to keep from starving. A study of the suicide rate in 1885 revealed that in France, the urban suicide rate was 263 per 1 million inhabitants, compared to 172 per million in the rural areas. In Belgium the urban suicide rate was nearly twice the rural.

Death from one cause or another was the

Above: This Italian knife-grinder was one of many Londoners who made their living in the city streets. Right: Birmingham, England, in 1886. The bird's-eye view shows the profusion of architectural styles in which the Victorians delighted. The "Greek temple" at right (the Town Hall) represents one popular tendency; the pseudo-French building another; the "gothic" monuments in the foreground yet another.

constant companion of the urban poor. In 1842 a British civil servant, Edwin Chadwick, published *A Report on the Sanitary Conditions of the Labouring Population*. This report was filled with shocking revelations. One of the things Chadwick discovered was that "of all who are born of the labouring classes in Manchester, more than 57 per cent die before they reach five years of age." Comparing the populations of Manchester and of the agricultural county of Rutland, he found that among the Rutlandshire farm laborers and their families the average life expectancy at birth was 38 years of age, while among the factory workers and their families it was only 17. Although the factory

workers earned more, this relative advantage was offset by their unwholesome environment. A poor diet, polluted water, filthy air, and extreme overcrowding made them prey to all sorts of diseases, especially the contagious ones. Every year, typhoid, smallpox, and tuberculosis killed thousands of people in Britain. Tuberculosis was the greatest killer of the three, claiming victims chiefly among young people.

The steady, year-in, year-out loss of life caused little alarm among the authorities. But the great cholera epidemic of 1831-33 shocked the country. This disease raged throughout Britain and eventually killed 60,000 people. No one knew what caused the

disease or exactly how it spread, but it clearly had something to do with the conditions in which people lived. And it was the filthiest slums that had the greatest number of fatalities.

Various reports, including the one by Chadwick, gave statistical evidence of the connection between unsanitary conditions and the spread of disease. They urged the adoption of certain basic preventive measures, such as cleaning up the water supply, and the establishment of a national board of health. Chadwick argued that it would cost the cities less to provide a decent house for a working man than it cost to support families left destitute through the death of the head of the household. Such economic arguments generally carried more weight with a government elected by the propertied classes than did purely moral arguments. The next few decades saw the gradual acceptance of the idea that the government had a responsibility to maintain certain standards of hygiene. Parliament passed a number of Acts—not without vigorous opposition from some members—providing for such things as proper ventilation in factories, compulsory smallpox vaccination, and the pasteurization of milk.

Throughout the 1800s many middle- and upper-class people clung to the callous belief that the poor deserved their misfortune because they were "sinful." But here and there, thoughtful people took a different viewpoint and tried to do something positive about improving the lot of the lower classes.

Some enlightened industrialists were very concerned about the conditions in which their workers lived. One of these was the British mill owner Robert Owen. Between 1800 and 1820 Owen established a town for

Right: Leeds Town Hall, opened in 1858, reflects the self-conscious civic pride of the booming industrial towns and also the current taste for the grandiose. In spirit, it resembles some of the post-war "wedding-cake" buildings of the USSR.

Below: *Pentonville Road,* painted by John O'Connor in 1881. In the background rise the spires of St. Pancras Station and Hotel. The foreground, with its smart carriages and horse-drawn buses, has a cheerful aspect, reminding one that city life in the 1800s was not entirely as Doré saw it.

workers in his cotton mill in Lanarkshire, Scotland. Owen's intent was to make New Lanark a community of "industry, temperance, comfort, health, and happiness." To this end, he improved the workers' housing, shortened working hours in his factory, gave unemployment relief when there wasn't enough work, opened a store where people could buy goods at near cost price, and placed strict supervision on the sale of liquor. He refused to employ young children in his mill, and, instead, provided free schooling for them.

New Lanark attracted visitors from all over Europe, who were impressed by the well-being of its inhabitants as well as by the commercial success of the mill. Owen hoped ultimately to reorganize society into thousands of small communities similar to New Lanark. Because of his opposition to the organized religions, however, he could not get much support from influential people in Britain. So he went to the United States, where, in 1825, he tried to establish a co-operative community called New Harmony, in Indiana. Many people were interested, but most of those who joined him there were

123

idle or impractical. This experiment in community living never got underway, and Owen lost a great deal of money.

Another industrialist and social reformer was Titus Salt. In 1853, near Bradford, Salt opened the massive woolen mill already mentioned. Once the mill was established, he set about building an ideal town—called "Saltaire"—for its workers. An orderly grid of streets was laid out, and 850 workers' dwellings were built in small terraces. Although similar to the conventional bye-law houses of the day, these were somewhat larger. And the streets were wider. In one corner of the town the managers had their larger houses, set in gardens.

Titus Salt's concern for his workers' well-being did not stop with their housing. He provided public wash houses, a school, an infirmary, almshouses, a club and institute, and a public park. Like many reformers of the 1800s, he regarded alcohol as a major evil, and so the little town was "dry." He built several churches and encouraged faith-ful attendance by his employees. Culture and recreation were not forgotten: the town had a library and reading room, a billiard hall, and allotments, where people could grow their own vegetables.

Other model towns were built elsewhere in Britain and other industrialized countries. In Germany, the Krupp family of steel and munitions manufacturers built towns for their workers outside Essen. In 1867, an American industrialist George M. Pullman, designer of the railroad car named for him, built a model town for his employees. Located near Chicago, Pullman City had running water and sewage disposal, good houses, shops, and a cultural center that included a library and a theater.

All of these communities offered living conditions significantly better than those in the large cities. But they were small towns, directed by one employer for his own workers. The major cities were complex social agglomerations where the law of

Above: This grim cartoon from *Punch*, in 1850, represented "a drop of London water" as seen through a microscope. It called attention to the pollution of London well water by drainage from graveyards.
Right: Titus Salt's model town, Saltaire, with its woolen mill and (at right) rows of workers' houses.

124

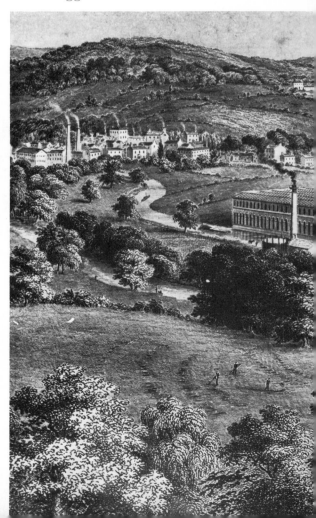

supply and demand was allowed to function freely and where every member of the "labor supply" had to fend for himself. Labor unions were slowly and painfully coming into existence in Europe and America, but their gains did not yet affect the vast majority of the working class.

In America, competition for jobs and housing became acute as millions of immigrants from Europe poured into the cities. Some of the immigrant groups, notably the Scandinavians, settled out in the country and farmed the land. But most of the people stayed in the cities, where they had friends and relatives and could keep their sense of community. Soon the cities became collections of ghettos—Irish, Italian, Russian, Jewish—each with its own character and color, but all sharing the ills of poverty and overcrowding.

The housing shortage in New York was especially severe. In 1850, just after the first great wave of Irish immigration, there were in New York 29,000 people living in cellars.

As late as the 1880s, the whole East Side from 42nd to 110th Street was an Irish shanty-town, where goats and pigs roamed the streets.

The crucial need, in such a situation, was not for new towns but for humanitarian work within the existing cities. The Salvation Army, founded in England in 1865, came to the United States in 1879. It provided a variety of social services, ranging from employment bureaus to cheap lodgings for vagrants. By this time, the humanitarian movement was well underway: in Philadelphia alone there were more than 800 charitable agencies.

The settlement house was one innovation in caring for the poor. The first of these, Toynbee Hall, was founded in London in 1884. Five years later, in Chicago, a young woman named Jane Addams opened another, called Hull House. Located on a busy street, between an undertaker's and a saloon, Hull House quickly attracted people from the surrounding Italian, German,

Bohemian, and Polish and Russian Jewish neighborhoods. Among the services offered at Hull House were a nursery and kindergarten for the children of working mothers, reading and sewing groups, and a coffee-room where people could come in the evening to visit. Today, such activities seem quite unremarkable, but in those days, they were innovations. Jane Addams believed in encouraging the immigrants to maintain their traditions. Certain evenings were devoted to programs of Italian and German culture. Handicrafts, such as spinning and weaving, were taught and displayed by the immigrant women. The weekly meetings of the "Working People's Social Science Club" gave people a chance to hear and discuss some of the political and economic ideas then gaining currency.

In her book *Twenty Years at Hull House*, Jane Addams indignantly described some of the conditions then existing in Chicago:

"The policy of the public authorities of never taking initiative . . . is obviously fatal in a neighbourhood where there is little initiative among the citizens. . . . The streets are inexpressibly dirty, the number of schools inadequate, sanitary legislation unenforced, the street lighting bad and altogether lacking in the alleys and smaller streets, and the stables foul beyond description."

Garbage was deposited in big wooden boxes fastened to the pavement, which were emptied very infrequently. "They were the first objects that the toddling child learned to climb," observed Miss Addams. "Their bulk offered a barricade and their contents provided missiles in all the battles of the older boys." Miss Addams had incinerators installed in the neighborhood. In the first two summers at Hull House she provided three baths in the house for the use of the neighborhood. A short time later, the first public bath in Chicago was built nearby.

Disposing of garbage and sewage is a staggering task for a large city. In the 1880s, port cities, such as New York and Boston,

Right: This painting of people awaiting admission to the casualty ward of a hospital is by the Victorian artist Luke Fildes. The melodramatic style of painting—extremely popular at the time—has a certain journalistic validity here, for the medical care available to the poorer classes was generally inadequate to meet the needs of a large, under-nourished, and disease-prone urban population.

Left: A room in Chicago's Hull House, which was the settlement house founded by Jane Addams in 1889. The settlement house was a community center, where poor people —particularly immigrants— could bring their problems, attend classes in useful skills, and take part in recreational activities with their neighbors.

disposed of garbage by taking it out to sea in barges and dumping it. Inland cities fed it to farm animals. The former system not only polluted the sea water, but also occasionally polluted the beaches. The latter system had the potential danger of causing trichinosis, a disease contracted by eating infected pork. After the 1880s cities began to burn their garbage or bury it.

Throughout the century, large cities began to construct underground sewers. London completed an extensive sewer system between 1856 and 1875. Its 83 miles of main sewer served an area of more than 100 square miles. But this system, like others of its time, did not treat the sewage it collected, but simply dumped it into the river. Not until the late 1800s were effective methods of sewage purification developed and adopted. But even today, some towns and cities still dump raw sewage into nearby waters.

Purification of water for drinking was also a long time coming. The citizens of St. Louis, Missouri, drank water from the Mississippi, after first letting the water stand in jars to allow the dirt to settle. As it became clear that many diseases were spread through contaminated water, cities gradually began paying attention to the quality of their water supply. New York led the way, opening the Croton Reservoir and Aqueduct in 1842. But many cities were slow to follow. As late as the 1880s the citizens of Chicago and Philadelphia were drinking contaminated water. The penalty for this negligence was demonstrated when, in that decade, twice as many people, proportionately, died from typhoid fever in Chicago and Philadelphia as died in New York and Boston, where the water was purified. Today, the industrialized countries have developed very efficient methods of purifying their water, and citizens need not fear such waterborne diseases as typhoid and cholera. Now that human health is fairly well safeguarded, people are finally turning their attention to other species, which suffer disease and death inflicted by industry. The millions of dead fish floating in the streams and lakes of Europe and North America are mute evidence of the menace that "Coketown" still poses to life on our planet.

Technical progress did bring some benefit to the city dweller. The steamship and improved methods of refrigeration greatly improved people's diet. Fresh vegetables and tropical fruits were available in mid-winter. One of the attractions at the Chicago Fair of 1893 was a then exotic food, the grapefruit. By contrast, the winter diet of rural people in northern parts of the United States was monotonous and generally less nutritious.

Eventually, improved diet and better medical care produced healthier citizens. One sign of this improvement was that

This large frame house, with its fancy Victorian trim, is typical of those built in America around 1900, when the move to the suburbs—made easier by better public transport—got underway. This one is in Westchester County, outside New York.

An early design for an underground rapid transit system for New York City featured cylindrical cars that would, theoretically, be pushed through the tubular tunnels by blasts of air. The picture (1874) shows the view from the tunnel into the station, with the train arriving. Thirty years later, the New York subway (quite different) was opened.

during the 1880s, American clothing stores began to stock more large sizes to meet the increased average size of their customers.

Urban congestion was alleviated by developments in public transport. Until the coming of the bus, trolley, and subway, the worker had to live within walking distance of his job. Now, the situation was changing.

Buses began to appear in cities in the early part of the century. Being horsedrawn and relatively small, they were only a partial solution. The trolley-car, first adopted by Richmond, Virginia, in 1887, was fast, comfortable, and cheap. For smaller cities, it seemed the ideal solution, but the big cities required something on a larger scale. An urban railway was the answer, but it clearly had to run either above the already-crowded streets or below them. New York built an elevated railway, which by 1881 was transporting 175,000 passengers a day. But the "El" was (and is) ugly and noisy, and it scattered dirt on pedestrians below it.

London was the first city to take its urban transport underground. Its Metropolitan Line opened in 1863. The steam locomotives that pulled these trains made the atmosphere in the Underground rather oppressive, and the development of electric locomotives around 1890 was a distinct improvement. Other cities followed London, and soon electrically run subways were operating in Budapest, Paris, Berlin, Boston, and New York.

The growth of a mass transit network made it possible for workers to live farther away from their jobs. Land in the suburbs was cheaper and, consequently, so was housing. By the turn of the century, the suburbs of New York had a total population of more than one million. The city could now spread out over the land as it never had before. The industrial city remained— but the congestion was eased. Many factories moved to the outskirts of towns. The suburbs became a goal that many could hope to reach. As the 20th century opened, few could predict that this escape would radically change the form of the western city, or that it would be a mixed blessing.

The face of Manhattan.
Gleaming glass giants such
as these proclaim the wealth
and power concentrated in a
great metropolis and belie the
poverty, violence, corrup-
tion, and decay that threaten
at times to destroy it.

Super City

6

THE MODERN WESTERN CITY has advantages hardly dreamed of a century ago. It has paving and sidewalks, electric lights, hot and cold running water (safe to drink), central heating and air conditioning, underground telephone wires, and indoor plumbing. It is a shiny place of glass-fronted office buildings and hotels, of lavishly decorated department stores, of immaculate hospitals, of swiftly gliding elevators and gently clicking computers, of vast automatic switchboards pulsating with messages. It resembles the city of yesterday as the jet plane resembles the covered wagon.

Looking at this list of material advantages we might think that after 5,000 years of practice man has perfected the city. But this is far from the case. Anyone who lives or works in a typical American or European city today knows that, despite its advantages, the modern city is beset with problems. As more and more people live in cities, the problems will become more pressing. Already, they often seem nearly insoluble to the people who grapple with them—the politicians, architects, social workers, economists, and city planners.

Among the questions to which the planners must find answers are: How can people be housed at reasonable cost? How can they get in and out of the city quickly and safely? How can the remaining bits of countryside be saved from the gluttony of the bulldozer? How can the city be made less noisy, less polluted, less crime-infested? How can a neighborhood be stopped from decaying, or from being overwhelmed by traffic?

The city of tomorrow will grow out of the city of today. It will probably continue some of the present trends and react against others. Before we can speculate on what sort of city will emerge, we need to understand, if only in general terms, some of the forces operating in the city we already know.

The 19th-century industrial city grew up partly as a result of the diminishing need for farmers. The majority of men, freed from the land, switched to producing manufactured goods. Later in the century the number of farmers decreased even further, mainly because machinery was taking over from manpower and horsepower. Today, only about 5 per cent of the people of the United States work on the land. In Great Britain, the percentage is even smaller: 3.2 per cent. But the number of people working in manufacturing has not increased very much. Recently, automation has taken over many of the jobs that formerly were done by workers. The big expansion has been in what are known as service industries. These include the work of such people as shopkeepers, postmen, clerks, teachers, and administrators. In the United States today more than half the working population is employed in such service industries.

Part of the increase came in the middle of the 1880s with the improvement of social services. Compulsory education created a sudden demand for more teachers. Improved medical care needed more nurses and other hospital staff. The civil service grew enormously. As governments became more involved in the lives of citizens, they required great armies of bureaucrats to run the various agencies. In 1793, Britain's Treasury Department employed only 37 people. Today, it employs about 2,500. Louis XIV housed his entire government in one wing of Versailles. Today, the French Ministry of Education alone employs 25,000 people.

The expansion in government has a parallel in business and in industry. The office worker and the office building have become the major elements in the new cities. This fact is so familiar today that we hardly realize what a recent development it is. In the 18th century, commercial life was so unspecialized that merchants ran their businesses from their own houses. One room at street level would be sufficient as a counting house. The East India Company was one of the biggest business concerns in 18th-century England; yet for the first 126 years of its existence it was run entirely from the private houses of its directors. Only in 1726 did they build a separate headquarters.

In the 1800s, factories had clerks, bookkeepers, and, of course, managers, but these relatively few people normally worked in the factory itself. It was only toward the end of the century that the scale of businesses grew so great that large and separate offices were required. When factories began to move out of town, the office stayed in the center. In town, businessmen could more easily maintain contact with related businesses, retailers, bankers, shippers, and insurance companies. They could also enjoy the city's attractions, such as good restaurants and theaters.

Various machines speeded up the work done in the office. In turn, they created more work. A sort of "Parkinson's Law" seems to have developed: the paperwork expanded to fit the machines provided for doing it. The memorandum and the report—their dictation, typing, copying, and filing—assumed a larger and larger part of the working day. The invention of the telephone and the typewriter, around 1880, created many new jobs—mostly filled by women.

Along with the change in work patterns came a change in the appearance of the city. Offices needed more space, but land in the city center was becoming expensive. So people built upward.

Formerly, the height of a building had been limited by the thickness of its walls. If a building was very high, then much of the ground area would be covered by the base of the wall. The apartment houses of ancient Rome that had fallen down did so because their walls were too thin. The Gothic cathedrals relied on buttresses, to support their stained-glass-filled walls.

When iron began to be used in construction, some builders realized that it might lend itself to multi-story buildings. In 1845, in New York, a building was erected in which the weight was taken entirely on cast-iron columns. By the 1870s iron was in common use in stores and factories. But the use of iron or steel in very tall buildings had to wait for the development of the electrically

Far left: Office work is the major activity of a modern city, and the design of offices is a complex matter involving aesthetics and psychology and a host of physical data. This German office has an "open plan" type of design.
Left: A traffic jam on London's Oxford Street. Part of the street is now reserved for taxis and buses, and the sidewalks are widened for the benefit of pedestrians.
Below: Air pollution in New York City.

powered elevator, capable of lifting people considerable heights, and for a municipal supply of electricity that would make such elevators generally practicable.

By the 1880s these conditions were being met, and the skyscraper made its first, rather modest, appearance, not in New York, but in America's second city, Chicago. The Mutual Bank Building was only 10 stories high, but its construction was quite revolutionary. It was built on a steel skeletal frame. The outer walls were, in effect, just skin around a cage; the steel girders and uprights held the building up.

Other office blocks grew up around it. Many of these were elegantly furnished. In 1893 a New York writer for *Harper's Magazine* described "their floors of deftly laid mosaic work, their walls of marble and onyx, their balustrades of copper . . . their artistic lanterns, elegant electric fixtures. . . ."

133

He concluded—in true New York fashion: "These Chicago office buildings force an exclamation of praise, however unwillingly it comes. . . ."

The office building is the monument of the 20th-century city, just as the cathedral, the palace, and the factory were the monuments of earlier cities. The gilded extravagance of the early office buildings has now given way to gleaming metal and glass, but the trend toward height, set by the first steel-frame buildings, has continued to produce office blocks of increasingly spectacular size. In the first half of the century, New York's financial district acquired the most breathtaking skyline in the world. Today the building boom has moved north to midtown Manhattan. This part of the city is in a perpetual state of upheaval, as glass and steel slabs rise up seemingly overnight. Shops, hotels, and office buildings that have an average age of only 40 or 50 (considered ancient in America) are destroyed to make way for these gleaming giants. Dust and debris from demolition sites fills the air, mingling with industrial and automotive pollutants to create New York's distinctive brown sky.

Some modern office buildings house enough workers to populate a small town. New York's Pan Am building, which contains nearly $2\frac{1}{2}$ million square feet of office space, is occupied by 25,000 workers. The new World Trade Center, whose twin towers are 1,350 feet high (surpassing the Empire State Building by 100 feet), has 9 million square feet of office space—enough to accommodate about 90,000 people.

This concentration of people and activities into a small area creates problems. Even to bring 25,000 people to one building at 9 A.M. and to disperse them at 5 P.M. is no easy job. Multiply this by the number of other skyscrapers, small offices, and shops in the area, and the task becomes monumental. Feeding all these people at lunchtime is another enormous undertaking, as the long lines in restaurants testify. Providing light, heat, and air-conditioning for the offices, maintaining

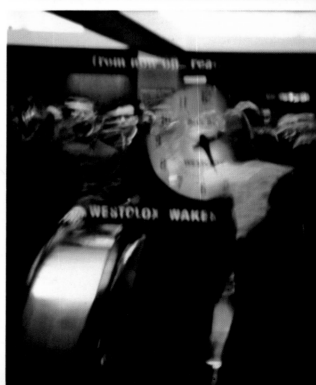

Above: Spring in Central
Park. Green space is very
important in a city as
overwhelming as New
York. Distance and foliage
lend extra beauty to the
spectacular skyline, and
the chance to be alone (or
relatively alone) for a while
makes it easier to return to
the pushing, hurrying
crowds—at left, Grand
Central Station at the
evening rush hour.
Right: "Tear it down, dig
it up, build something
else," is the continual story
in the big cities. Bigger
buildings bring more rent.
The low skyline of London
is changing, as more and
more skyscrapers go up.

their telephone service, and collecting their wastes are some of the other jobs done by armies of city workers.

The high density of the business districts of modern cities has not only created administrative headaches for city governments; it has also created a seemingly insoluble economic dilemma. Land at the center of the city is precious because it is the most accessible for everyone. This is why it is tempting to make very intensive use of it. But by building skyscrapers, the developers have actually increased the value of the land they are using, and so they create a vicious circle of rising prices and rising value.

Because land in the city center is so expensive, very few apartments, and even fewer houses, are built there. In central London today, 60 per cent of the land is covered by offices, over 17 per cent by warehouses, over 7 per cent by industry, and only a little over 1 per cent by houses or apartments. Many of the town houses built in earlier days have now been turned into offices. Only businesses or rich people can afford the high rents and the property taxes on them.

This is one reason behind the separation of workplace and home that we find in the modern western city. New Yorkers who might prefer to live in midtown Manhattan, close to offices, shops, and theaters, just can't afford to do so. This is particularly true of families with several children. They must, instead, look for homes in one of the other boroughs, or in neighboring New Jersey.

But the move away from the city center began—and continues—for another reason. Many people *want* to leave the city. They crave a bit of green, fresh air, space for their children to play, and, increasingly, safety.

Suburbs of one kind or another have been a feature of the city for a long time. Some medieval maps show "suburbs" clustering outside the walls of a town. Here lived some traders and various "non-acceptable" people—for example, the Welsh who lived outside the walls of Caernarvon.

But it wasn't until cities began to be very overcrowded and unhealthy—particularly during the Industrial Revolution—that suburban life became desirable. Prosperous people, who had carriages to take them around, moved out into the country, where they built large houses in spacious grounds. Many of these people were the owners of the mills whose soot and filth made the industrial city such an unpleasant place to live in. The great mass of the people, having no form of

Right: A suburban scene near San José, California. Each family has its own house, but little real space. Many city planners want to replace this land-wasteful type of development with higher density building, such as town houses surrounded by large areas of parkland.

Left: A street in central London at night. Tourism and entertainment keep some parts of London busy after dark, but much of the city is necessarily devoted to business, as few people can afford to live in the center. Most people who work in cities go home to suburbia at night.

transport other than their feet, continued to live in the city, crowded together around the factories and offices. Public transport changed this. The bus, streetcar, and subway not only gave people more mobility within the city but also gave them the freedom to choose where they would live. A great many of them chose the suburbs.

The early suburbs followed the railroads. The towns and villages served by trains from the city began to grow. But they remained separate communities. The amount of "sprawl" was checked by the fact that there would be only one station serving a community, and no one wanted to live a great distance away from it. The steam locomotive required at least a mile to achieve a fair speed, and so the towns and stations tended to be some distance apart. Subway and elevated trains, which run on electricity, could accelerate much more quickly, and their stations were built at more frequent intervals. The streetcar stopped very frequently, and so suburban development along the streetcar lines tended to take the shape of a ribbon.

These various kinds of transportation radiated out from the city like the spokes of a wheel. As they moved farther out, they also moved farther away from each other.

Green wedges were left between the "spokes." When the automobile came into general use, this pattern began to dissolve. People with cars did not have to settle near the railroad, streetcar, or subway. They could live anywhere in the suburban area. The green gaps were filled in. One suburb merged with another, and the whole developed area continued to spread outward. Suburban "sprawl" had arrived. Today, the sprawl has grown to such an extent that the suburbs of one city are meeting the suburbs of another.

Having started as rather exclusive communities, the suburbs began to change character as middle-income people moved in. These people could not afford the large lots and large houses of the first suburbanites. So they compromised.

In Britain, the compromise took the form of the semi-detached house, or duplex. These are two houses built together so as to resemble one large one. Originally, the idea may have been to suggest the manor houses of the landed gentry (although the difference between the two is readily apparent). Typically, the "semi" is built on a small lot, Britain being a country where land is scarce. The small but luxuriant gardens lend color to the scene, and the developers have tried to duplicate a bit of the romantic past by building in imitation historical styles such as mock-Tudor and neo-Georgian. The curving streets of many suburbs are another attempt to create a feeling of variety and spontaneity in the suburban landscape.

Despite such attempts, the overwhelming characteristic of the typical suburb is its sameness. A common theme of pre-World War II cartoonists in Britain and America was the distress of the homecoming commuter unable to recognize his own house.

The American suburb differs from its British counterpart by consisting almost entirely of detached houses. The effect is somewhat more open, with slightly larger lots and very few garden walls. But few of the lots are sufficiently large to afford much privacy for the owners. The houses may be separate, but many of them are so close that next-door neighbors can almost shake hands by leaning out of their windows.

Still, the suburbanite can at least play his hi-fi, or operate an electric drill, without his neighbor banging on the wall—which cannot be said of the tenant of a modern thin-walled "luxury" apartment in town. And if the suburbanite has not achieved country living, he at least has a patch of green where his children can play and he and his wife can sit on a summer evening.

The evidence seems to indicate that most people (in English-speaking countries, at least) prefer the suburbs to the city as a place to live. A survey of dock workers in Portsmouth, England, revealed that 80 per cent of them would rather travel up to 30 minutes to work and have their own houses than live in apartments near their jobs. A similar preference exists in the higher income brackets. Many business executives will spend two hours or more each day imprisoned in nerve-racking traffic or in the antiquated coaches of a commuter train in order to live in a fashionable "exurb."

Located beyond the main mass of the suburbs, often 30 miles or more from the city, these exurbs offer more space and something approaching a small-town atmosphere. But, like the suburbs, they are mainly residential. In fact, in the United States they're often called "bedroom communities." For the tired commuter jogging along toward

Above: Dream house, English style—a thatched cottage far from the big, noisy, dirty city. The automobile and a good system of commuter trains make it possible for many Englishmen to have their homes 25 miles or more from their work in town.

Right: Dream house, American style. The ranch-style house—long, low, and set on a large lot—is the typical habitat of the affluent, middle-class American. With two or more cars, the family has easy mobility. In expensive suburbs like this, trees are spared by the builders, and owners can enjoy a bit of nature.

Westport or Grosse Pointe on the 5:52, his destination is mainly a place to eat and sleep—a sort of "refueling station" where he prepares to meet the demands of the following day. For his wife and children, however, the "bedroom community" is a full-time home. What sort of home is it?

In many ways the exurb—and the suburb—are very desirable places to live. Besides the fresh air and green spaces, they offer relative safety from crime, better schools, and recreation facilities that used to be found only in the city. The shopping center, once a purely functional and un-

inviting row of shops, has (particularly in the United States) blossomed into a dazzling, multilevel assortment of shops and services, good restaurants, and plazas with fountains and places to sit and relax. Suburbs formerly lacking any focal point now have one. The shopping center is worth watching as the nucleus of towns of tomorrow.

The low density of the suburbs means that people who live there are very dependent on the automobile. Many a suburban housewife spends half her day chauffeuring the family around: her husband to the station in the morning, herself to the supermarket and then to the hairdresser's, the children to dancing class and Cub Scouts, her husband back from the station in the evening.

Her counterpart in the city can walk to the supermarket just around the corner or even to the department store ten blocks away. If the weather is bad, she can take a bus or taxi. Driving a car in the city tends to be more trouble and expense than it is worth. In the suburbs, where buses and taxis are almost nonexistent, distances greater, and parking space abundant, people drive as a matter of course. In fact, they have now acquired the habit of using the car to go anywhere, even to the drugstore three blocks away. Anyone who walks for recreation is considered eccentric. In parts of suburban Los Angeles, a pedestrian is likely to be approached by a suspicious police officer and questioned.

The automotive way of life encouraged by the suburbs not only robs people of the physical benefits of walking, but also deprives them of close contact with their environment

A place to park the car is one big advantage of the shopping center. Once inside, the shopper can stroll from one store to another, often in climatically controlled arcades, without the bother of crossing busy streets. Above: A big shopping center in Atlanta, Georgia. The design of shopping centers offers plenty of scope for imaginative architects. At left: An urban shopping center in Düsseldorf, Germany.

and with other human beings. By contrast, the sidewalks of Fifth Avenue on a Sunday afternoon are full of people—New Yorkers, tourists, and suburbanites in search of activity. Some of the people are on their way to Rockefeller Center to ice skate, or just to watch other people skate; some are going to the Museum of Modern Art to look at the works of Picasso; others are going to St. Thomas's Church next door to listen to Bach; still others are heading toward Central Park to look at tigers and polar bears. Window-shopping at Tiffany's and Bonwit Teller can be indulged in, safe from the temptation to buy. People-watching can be indulged in to the heart's content.

Few city centers are as lively on a Sunday as is midtown Manhattan. New York's weekend and nighttime vitality is maintained partly by its relatively large residential population and partly by its constant flow of visitors (although the vitality is declining because many people are scared away by the city crime). The resident population is a major factor in keeping many European cities so active. In Vienna, for example, roughly one quarter of the area inside the Ringstrasse (the boulevard on the site of the old city walls) is occupied by houses and apartments, some above shops. This relatively high proportion of residential building helps to make the center of Vienna lively almost around the clock.

London, a much larger, more sprawling city than Vienna, has pockets of weekend and evening activity in the center, especially during the tourist season. But one section of London, the City, illustrates dramatically the trend toward after-business-hours slump

in the modern city. In 1831, this area, covering slightly more than one square mile, had a population of 125,000. Today, this has shrunk to 4,000. On a weekday morning, some 1¾ million people pour into the City to work. At night, they disperse, and the City becomes the province of cats and caretakers.

After working hours, many American city streets have little or nothing to attract people. Moreover, the rising crime rate in these streets acts as a positive deterrent. In the past few years, even businesses have begun to move out of the centers. Victor Gruen, an architect and city planner, describes in his book *The Heart of Our Cities* a few signs of decline he has observed in the core areas of several American cities.

One of these is Cincinnati, Ohio. In 1940, downtown Cincinnati's daytime population (people working and shopping) was 11,500.

Right: Parts of New York retain a strong community spirit. This "block party" in Greenwich Village has been organized by a neighborhood association to raise money for some extra street amenities. The police have closed the street to traffic, and people can wander among the stalls and even dance to the music of a rock band. Although the owners and many of the tenants of these buildings are prosperous, rent control enables many long-established families of modest means to stay on in this fashionable area.

By 1960 this had dwindled to 6,500. In 1948 the area had 1,054 retail establishments; 10 years later it had only 854.

"These dry statistics [says Gruen] are reflected in the poor appearance and the lifelessness of the city core, in the numerous FOR RENT signs on stores and office buildings, in the large vacancy rate of hotel rooms, in a downgrading of the quality and character of the stores still doing business, in the closing of many theaters and movie houses, in the emptiness of streets at night and on holidays and Sundays . . . in the neglected appearance of buildings and stores and in a general deterioration of the environmental qualities."

Poverty and its companions, crime, disease, and drug addiction, are the most baffling and serious problems facing the city today. They are certainly far from new problems in the history of the city. What *is* new is the urgency we feel about solving them. Part of the urgency is our developing social conscience; part is simply well-founded fear. In many American cities, generations of racial prejudice and inequality have begun to yield a harvest of violence. The despair of the ghetto is a bitter mockery of the shiny, glittering office buildings and elegant hotels that symbolize our prosperity.

In an attempt to improve the physical environment of the poor, the city tears down the slums and puts up public housing. Generally, this takes the form of high-rise buildings, surrounded by plots of grass. They represent a physical improvement over the vermin-infested slums they replace, but on the whole they have not been successful. Their impersonal, anonymous quality seems to break down whatever sense of community people had in their run-down, but noisy and colorful, streets. The stairwells and elevators lend themselves to vandalism and crime.

The people who live in the housing projects often show indifference to keeping them neat, an attitude that middle-class people find difficult to understand. A clue to the reason for their indifference emerges in Jane Jacobs' book *The Death and Life of Great American Cities*. Mrs. Jacobs, a sharp critic of housing projects, tells how a certain project in East Harlem had a large lawn, which the tenants particularly hated. They said it was useless and should be destroyed. A social worker was baffled by their hostility to a harmless patch of grass until one day one of the tenants exploded:

For these children, living in a slum in Spanish Harlem, New York is a prison. They share their cell with cockroaches and rats. Later, the older inmates will initiate them into the ways of gang warfare and heroin addiction. In the 200 years since Hogarth depicted Gin Lane, city life has not changed much for the people at the bottom.

" 'Nobody cared what we wanted when they built this place. They threw our houses down and pushed us here and pushed our friends somewhere else. We don't have a place around here to get a cup of coffee or a newspaper even, or borrow fifty cents. Nobody cared what we need. But the big men come and look at that grass and say, "Isn't it wonderful! Now the poor have everything!" ' "

While some city neighborhoods decay into slums, others are so lively and attractive that they become fashionable and expensive. The west part of Greenwich Village, New York, is an example. It used to be inhabited by many struggling young artists and lower income families. Today, the artists are successful ones, and the families are those of stockbrokers and lawyers. The struggling artists have moved into the east part of the Village, where the houses are plainer and the rents are lower.

Nesta Roberts, a British journalist living in Paris, reports on the neighborhood she lives in, which is experiencing a subtle transformation. Within the 81 houses that line her street live 1,042 people, including 625 who work. The employed people include 10 managing directors, 38 shop assistants, 15 architects, 3 policemen, 15 journalists, and 54 laborers. The apartments are rented according to what Miss Roberts calls "vertical democracy."

The rents drop as storeys rise, so that, under the eaves of an apartment whose first floor houses a fashionable doctor or a musician with a national and international reputation, there may be a former waiter on his pension, or the friendly slightly disorientated old lady who comes out daily in a pink dressing gown to talk to her own and other people's

145

cats, and to sweep the pavement for several yards on either side of her door.

Up to about eight years ago it was possible to satisfy all needs of mind and body without leaving our street. . . . The rot began when the fish shop closed, and this at a period when fish on Fridays was still obligatory. There will never be another in our street, because four minutes away is a vast *prisunic* [a sort of combined dime store and supermarket] where trout swim in tanks. . . . Every time one of the elderly craftsmen or pensioners dies, or moves into an old people's home, the apartment is tarted up and let at an even higher rent to a tenant who is almost inevitably middle class.

Within the center of a city, there should be room for people of all classes and for a mixture of activities. But there is a great tendency for one kind of enterprise to "take over" an area to the exclusion of other functions. Sometimes this happens naturally, and sometimes it is made to happen by zoning laws. Many people—city-dwellers as well as suburbanites—cling to the idea of keeping residential streets purely residential. Yet some of our most thoughtful urban historians and city planners speak out vigorously in favor of mixed zones. Zoning laws, they feel, should be used only to keep out heavy industries that create smoke and excessive noise. Today, many industries that were once physically obnoxious have been cleaned up and made quieter by advances in technology, and so need not be banished to the city outskirts. It may be that the future will bring a "re-mixing" of people and activities in our cities.

Every weekday morning, high above the bridges and highways leading into New York, a helicopter hovers and circles. A man sitting beside the pilot scans the ground below and reports his observations into a microphone. And all over suburban New York, men sitting at their breakfast tables, putting on their coats, or backing their cars out of driveways listen intently to hear the bad news:

In an effort to preserve and restore the quality of city neighborhoods, local councils in Britain offer grants to house-owners to improve their property. Dilapidated shells of houses, such as the one at left, can be saved from the bulldozer (and replacement by an impersonal, shiny office block or apartment building) and transformed into gracious and comfortable homes. Part of the conversion cost must be paid by the owner, but the council will often lend him this money.

"Palisades Parkway very very heavy now. . . . We had a stalled car on the East River Drive a moment ago. . . ." And the occasional good news: "All lanes are open going from George Washington Bridge to midtown." Traffic has become a force like the weather. Even though man-made, it seems to have some irresistible power of its own. All the individual can do is try to avoid its worst moments. Traffic affects everyone who lives in the city, works in the city, or just passes through the city. And it raises blood pressure everywhere, from the seething Fiat-filled piazzas of Rome to the General Motorized arteries of Los Angeles.

For a long time now the city has been trying to cope with the automobile. Roads have been widened; traffic is "managed" so that much of it is one-way routes; circles and underpasses have been built. More drastically, highways have been built right through the city. Sometimes, as in Brussels, a highway is built on stilts, so that local traffic can carry on beneath it and on either side. The limited access elevated highway is a great help in moving traffic. For example, a motorist who needs to go from the Bronx, at the upper end of New York City, down to the Wall Street area, can take the East River Drive and Franklin D. Roosevelt Drive, or the West Side Highway. Either of these routes will take him to his destination without his having to join the stop-and-start parade of frustration in the city streets.

In theory it seems an ideal solution to at least one part of the traffic problem. And most of the time it works fairly well. Certainly even in rush hours, the traffic on these expressways moves a little less slowly than

Some Moslem cities are pilgrimage centers, the most famous being Mecca in Saudi Arabia, the birthplace of Mohammed. Such cities have hundreds of caravanserai—inns built around courtyards, where pilgrims are accommodated. A city such as Mecca derives much of its income from the trade of pilgrims. Religion is, in a sense, its most important "business." The same could be said of Lourdes, in France, or—in medieval times—of Canterbury.

Although Shiraz is not a pilgrimage center, it is definitely a religion-centered town. Its mosques are not only centers of worship, but also gathering-places where people can visit or simply sit and relax, away from the commotion of the streets.

Many Middle Eastern cities have a compact, enclosed form. This view of Mahan, Iran, shows the sharp distinction between city and country. In the foreground is the Shrine of Shah Nematullah Vali.

Running through the old town of Shiraz is the bazaar, a street of shops where tradesmen sell food, clothing, and a tremendous range of other items, both useful and ornamental. As in the European medieval market, the craftsmen are grouped according to craft: all the metalworkers are in one place, all the leather workers in another. Haggling over the price of an item is part of the shopping process, here as in other pre-industrial cities.

A few modern shops can be found in the old city. But most of the modern features of Shiraz are found beyond the former walls, where streets are wider, alleys fewer. Here we find a university, schools, a hospital, and office buildings, in addition to many new houses.

The original suburbs of Shiraz were simply communities of Christians (mainly Armenians) who were required to live out-

160

side the protection of the city walls. Moslem cities had, and still have, minorities of Jews, who were allowed to live in the city but confined to ghettos—some of which were walled. They formed, in a sense, a town within a town, just as they did in many European cities.

It is not surprising that there is some resemblance between Shiraz and the Old City of Delhi, the capital of India. For several centuries, Old Delhi was one of the strongholds of the Moguls, who invaded India in the early 1500s. Turks by race, the Moguls were Moslem by religion, and they brought to India some of the shapes and patterns that characterize the cities of Islam. The most famous building in India, the Taj Mahal, was built by a Mogul prince. The domes and minarets of the Middle East were copied, with subtle alterations, in the mosques of Old Delhi.

Side by side with crowded, wall-encircled Old Delhi is New Delhi, a striking example of how colonial expansion from Europe has changed the urban face of the rest of the world. This part of the city dates only from the early part of this century, when the British, who then governed India, moved the capital here from Calcutta.

New Delhi was planned by an Englishman, according to Renaissance ideas of town design. Its grand avenues, focusing on the palatial Residence of the governor, symbolized the might of the British Empire. Its spacious regularity made a striking contrast with the teeming, narrow streets of the old city.

This contrast between native and foreign is seen again and again in India, even in the smaller towns. The British used to establish themselves outside the old crowded towns in what were called "lines." These were areas

Left: Pilgrims thronged around the Kaaba in the city of Mecca—the focus of Moslem pilgrimage for over a thousand years. Below: A typical narrow street in Shiraz, Iran, leading to one of the city's many mosques.

Above: A typical narrow street in Old Delhi. Many of the buildings in Indian cities are a blend of western and eastern architecture. The State Government Secretariat building (right) in Bangalore, capital of Mysore, shows British influence in the imposing columns and Hindu influence in the fanciful and elaborate trim.

Right: The sacred city of Benares (now called Varanasi) on the River Ganges. Hindus from all over India come to this city to bathe in the river. The bathing (far right), called Puja, is believed to cleanse body and soul.

162

Right: A typical scene of want and squalor in the streets of Calcutta. Thousands of people, many with no home other than the street, must beg for their food, or—as these people are doing—search for it in a rubbish dump.

designated for certain segments of the population: "civil lines" for administrators, "military lines" for soldiers, and so on.

"Lines" was an apt name for these communities, for their streets were laid out in parallel lines, wide and tree-shaded. Adapting native Indian architecture to their own use, the British built row after row of *bungalows* with shaded *verandahs* (both Indian words), and set them back from the street in cool gardens. The British quarter also included the law courts and other government buildings, hospitals, schools, churches, and clubs. The "lines" had, at worst, a regimented, rigid quality, but at best, a feeling of order and spaciousness that comes as a relief after the congested native town.

Ironically, the most crowded and squalid

163

In Japanese cities eastern and western styles mingle to
produce a culture as different from the old Japan as it
is from the cities of the modern West.
Above: Traditionally-clad diners at an open-air
restaurant. Left: A Tokyo railway pusher squeezes
one last passenger into an overcrowded car.

city in India today was founded by these
space-loving British colonists. Calcutta,
located on the Hoogly River in the province
of Bengal, began its existence as a trading
center. Then, as now, the site was unhealthy,
but this was overlooked by the colonists
because it was such an excellent location for
trade. Eventually, Calcutta became the
capital of India, and remained so until 1912,
when the capital was moved to Delhi.

While it was the capital, Calcutta acquired
many fine government buildings. It has

sometimes been called "the city of palaces," a reference to the opulent mansions of its rich English merchants. But poverty, not palaces, is the hallmark of Calcutta today— poverty on a scale that westerners find hard to imagine. Even in the 19th century Calcutta had a bad reputation. In his poem "A Tale of Two Cities," Rudyard Kipling characterized it in these words:

As the fungus sprouts chaotic from its bed,
So it spread—
Chance-directed, chance-erected, laid and built
On the silt—
Palace, byre, hovel—poverty and pride—
Side by side—
And above the packed and pestilential town,
Death looked down.

Today, Calcutta has more than 3 million inhabitants (not including its metropolitan area). Of these people, 600,000 are homeless. Approximately one person out of every five lives, literally, in the street. In some parts of Calcutta, each person has an average of only five square yards of space. The countryside has its poverty (in fact, migration from the country is one cause of urban overcrowding), but in the cities the effects of poverty are aggravated by overcrowding. The lack of sanitation and proper food preservation, combined with oppressive heat most of the year, help to make Calcutta one of the most disease-ridden cities in the world. Bodies emaciated and disfigured by malnutrition, leprosy, cholera, or syphilis are a common sight in the streets of Calcutta.

The cities of India and Southern Asia differ from western cities in having many residents in the center. The center of a typical modern American or European city is almost empty of residents. In an eastern city, population density increases as one moves nearer the center. In smaller cities, merchants, shopkeepers, and craftsmen still live behind and above their business premises. In larger cities, poor newcomers often live in slums near the center.

Many Asian cities have grown to an enormous size. The Calcutta and Bombay conurbations each have nearly 5 million people; Seoul, the capital of South Korea, has 3.7 million; Shanghai 6.9 million; Tokyo, 11 million (the entire Tokyo-Yokohama metropolitan area has 14 million). Even more startling than the present size of these cities is the *rate* of growth in this part of the world. About 30 years ago, the "million" cities of the world were, with a few exceptions, located in the West. Now, most of them are in the developing countries, and some of them are doubling in size every 10 years. The prospect is frightening. In another generation Calcutta may have grown to 20 million people. It is bursting at the seams even now. One hesitates to imagine what it will be like then.

Even Tokyo, the capital of a rapidly industrializing nation that lacks India's severe poverty, is experiencing growing pains. Before this century only a minority of Japanese lived in the cities. But Tokyo itself has been a big city for some time; it may have had a million people two centuries ago, before the largest European city, London, reached that figure.

Once Japan became linked economically to the western world in the 1860s, Tokyo

165

began adopting modern innovations: steam trains, gaslight, electric power. Between the two World Wars, the city built a subway system. This system, with very few more recent extensions, must serve a population that has more than tripled since it was built. The crush on Tokyo's rush-hour trains makes the New York subway seem comfortable by comparison. An army of

Left: The city of Wusih, in China's Lower Yangtze Basin, is typical of the towns in this region in having a network of canals, which carry much of the city's freight. This tranquil scene of a canal crossed by a graceful arched bridge hardly suggests a city with growing industry and a population of some 600,000.

In countries where private cars are virtually non-existent, the bicycle is a popular form of transport—and it certainly takes up less room. Chinese city streets are full of cyclists at rush hours. Left: A typical scene at a station in Shanghai.

"pushers," stationed throughout the system, have the responsibility of ensuring that as many people as possible get into each car—and a few more besides.

Housing is still a major problem in Tokyo. There is a severe shortage of land and buildings, in the metropolitan area as well as in the congested center. Basic services are very inadequate. As late as the 1960s, two thirds of Tokyo households still had no sewerage, and had their waste collected at night by workmen. Much of this raw sewage was dumped into the Pacific Ocean.

In the heart of Tokyo, modern office buildings (but few skyscrapers, because of the threat of earthquakes) are mixed in with private houses and gardens, shops, and restaurants. One area, the Ginza, combines elegant shops with tawdry penny arcades, and at night its neon signs make it as gaudy as Times Square. Restaurants do a thriving business, thanks to the many Tokyo businessmen entertaining on expense accounts. The Japanese work hard and play hard, and Tokyo is a city that hums day and night.

Peking presents a striking contrast to the hurly-burly of Tokyo. In form, it has changed little since Marco Polo described it at the end of the 1200s. He observed that "the town is built in the form of a square," and that "the whole design of the town displays the greatest regularity and the streets are for this reason so straight that he who enters by one of the gates and gazes straight ahead sees the opposite gate at the other end of the town."

The center of Peking was, and still is, occupied by the Forbidden City, a complex of palaces and courtyards painted in brilliant colors and enclosed by a moat and a high rectangular wall. Peking's regularity is typical of the cities of northern China. Ch'ang-an was designed in much the same form. When the Chinese built a city they tried to reproduce what they thought was the plan of the universe. A city should be square in shape, because the earth was thought to be square. Its wall probably represented the mountains girdling the earth. And the wall—if the rules were strictly adhered to—would have 12 gates, one for each month of the year. The orientation of the city had to be exactly north, east, south, and west, and the principal buildings had always to face south.

China is a vast country, and there is tremendous variety among its cities. Teeming Shanghai, with its busy port and skyscrapers built earlier in the century by foreign entrepreneurs, has a European aspect. Peking, by contrast, has remained almost untouched by foreign influence.

Some of the picturesque aspects of Peking have disappeared under Communism. Formerly, much of the commerce in Peking was carried on by peddlars. There were peddlars who sold only thread, those who sold charcoal, those who sold turnips and radishes, those who sold pomegranate blossoms. Some of them cried their wares with the aid of Buddhist temple horns or kettles that they struck with sticks, making a cheerful din as they made their way through the narrow streets that lie behind the grand processional avenues. Street entertainers also enlivened pre-Communist Peking.

Today, the city has a curiously tranquil atmosphere. Joseph Kraft, an American correspondent who visited Peking during President Nixon's trip to China in 1972, voiced his impressions in an interview for the British Broadcasting Company. He commented, in particular, on the pace of Peking: "It isn't an urban pace . . . people move in the kind of slow deliberate way that one associates . . . with a rural setting. They bicycle very slowly. A lot of them are often just standing around and gossiping." One morning Kraft awoke early to find that it had snowed during the night. At about 6 A.M., he said, "there suddenly appeared in front of our hotel . . . several hundred people who with kind of makeshift brooms and little hoes began sweeping away the snow. . . . They weren't knocking themselves out. But there was a steady kind of work, and the snow was gone by the time we got up and started to get out. It's an example of massive utilization of manpower in a highly organized way, but without any of the kind of frenetic quality that . . . many outsiders have attached to life here in China."

Not surprisingly, the city has no frivolous entertainment, such as one finds in cities outside China. Kraft noticed the absence even of cafés: "There seems to be nowhere anybody can meet." Peking does have its theater and music—all carefully purged of western "decadent" influences—which are enthusiastically patronized by the Chinese people. Also, there are many parks and gardens and beautiful buildings, a legacy from Imperial rule, which lend color and charm to the life of Communist Peking.

Another part of the world that is experiencing a very rapid urban growth is Latin America. Here the population explosion is as severe as anywhere in Asia. In addition to the high birth-rate, there is a great movement of people from country to town, resulting in cities that are growing so quickly that planners cannot cope with the problem.

Latin America had cities, as we have seen, long before the Spanish and Portuguese arrived. The conquerors destroyed most of these Indian cities, but often kept the original sites when building their own cities, and sometimes retained something of the original street plans. Mexico City, for example, was built on the site of the Aztecs'

Spanish and Portuguese colonization in America produced cities that strongly resemble those of southern Europe. The Plaza de Armas (right) in Cuzco, Peru, shows the baroque spirit of the 1600s, particularly in the imposing cathedral at left. Below: The Tome Tagle Palace in Lima.

Tenochtitlán and followed to some extent the plan of the original capital.

But many of the colonial towns were built from scratch, on new sites. The European invaders depended for their lives on keeping contact with their homeland. So they favored sites near the coast. Cities such as Buenos Aires, Rio de Janeiro, and Lima were at first mere toe-holds on this vast, unexplored continent. They were islands of Spanish and Portuguese civilization from which the colonists could reach out to settle the new land and exploit its resources.

Most of these colonial towns were established in the 1500s, when Renaissance ideals

Open-air markets in the towns and cities attract farmers with their produce and also craftsmen with handmade goods. In the market of Latacunga, Ecuador, this Indian woman makes use of a sewing machine to do some on-the-spot sewing for a customer.

were flourishing in Europe. So it is not surprising that the centers of most Latin American towns and cities are very orderly and filled with impressive, often ornate, buildings: a cathedral, a viceroy's palace, and government buildings.

The planning of the towns was not left to the whims of individual settlers. In 1573, a list of Royal Ordinances, containing 149

rules for planning new towns, was sent from Spain to governors in the New World. The regulations made obligatory the grid pattern that had already been used for cities.

They further stipulated that the towns were to grow by extensions of the grid pattern, thus tidying up the messy little "suburbs" that tended to grow up around the edges. Town builders were to avoid irregular sites where the grid would be difficult to impose on the terrain. Widths of streets were specified according to practical considerations: where the climate was cool the streets would be wide; where it was hot, narrow—thus providing welcome shade in the more torrid parts of Central and South America. The central plaza, surrounded by public buildings, was an important element in the plan.

The original center of Caracas, Venezuela, is typical of Spanish colonial city planning. Its streets follow a grid plan laid down in 1578. The buildings in this area date from the 19th century (the original buildings having been destroyed by an earthquake), and include the cathedral, a one-story government building, shops, and houses. Adjacent to this area is the new Caracas, whose high-rise buildings reflect the country's recent prosperity.

As late as the beginning of this century, Caracas was a town of 50,000 inhabitants, the capital of a poor agricultural country. Then, in the 1920s, oil was discovered. Money poured into the country and transformed the rather provincial capital into a bustling metropolis. Today, the population of Caracas has passed the 2 million mark. Its streets are crammed with traffic; a wide multilane highway, running through the center of the new city, is a roaring river of cars from morning until night. With its gleaming white offices, apartments and hotels, and its dramatic setting—in the mountains near the sea—Caracas is an impressive and often beautiful city.

But there is another side to the picture. The visitor coming into this fine city from the airport must first pass through the *barrios*. These are the shantytowns that have grown up on the outskirts of Caracas.

Shantytowns are a common feature of many cities in the developing world. They are communities of squatters, who have moved in from the countryside onto land they do not own and claimed it by building shanties. A century ago, New York had shantytowns, in which Irish immigrants lived until they could get more permanent homes. Today shantytowns have disappeared from most western cities, whose suburbs are generally middle- or upper-class. (Rome is a striking exception; some 65,000 people, mostly from the rural south, are now living in shanties around the Italian capital.)

In Latin America, peasants are leaving the land, where there are too many mouths to feed, and moving to the cities in droves. Shantytowns are the result. In Santiago, Chile, they are known as *callampas;* in Buenos Aires, as *villas de miseria* (towns of misery). Certainly they have a miserable aspect. They consist of hundreds of shanties, called, ironically, *ranchos* (ranches). There are about 50,000 ranchos in Caracas; one

Shantytowns encircle many Latin American cities—and cities in other parts of the world as well. Below: Shanties outside the modern city of São Paulo, Brazil. Right: Houses in a workers' town in Brazil have a somewhat sturdier, more permanent appearance.

Caracas resident in five lives in a shanty.

The ranchos go up overnight. Some of them are no more than a few boxes or beaten-out oil drums nailed together and topped with a zinc roof. In the barrios there is often no sanitation and little water. In some cases there is electricity, because this is relatively easy to install once a barrio has grown up. Fortunately, the warm climate of Caracas makes brick walls unnecessary.

At first glance, one would call a barrio a slum. Certainly it resembles a slum in being dirty, unkempt, and crowded. But a real slum (and there are plenty of these in Caracas) is a place of old, decaying buildings, a place of despair. The barrio is different. Passing through it, one begins to see subtle improvements. Here a man is rebuilding his first rough shack with a zinc one; his next-door neighbor is rebuilding his in brick. In the midst of all the poverty and confusion a street is beginning to appear, not unlike some of those in old Caracas. The people are building a new life for themselves. Basically, the difference between a slum and a barrio is hope.

Still, the barrio is an eyesore and a worry to those who govern the city. In the 1950s the Caracas government made an effort to rehouse the rancho dwellers in new apartments. Thousands of ranchos were bulldozed, and new "super blocks" 15 stories high were built in their place. In four years 100,000 people were rehoused. But this massive building program meant jobs, and so more people were attracted to the city. While the 100,000 rancho dwellers were being rehoused, 160,000 more peasants moved to Caracas. There were more ranchos than ever.

Even assuming that rehousing could keep pace with immigration, it is far from an ideal solution. People who have lived in huts in the country all their lives are totally disoriented in a high-rise apartment building. More social problems are created than are solved.

Some people now think that the answer lies in helping the immigrants to build better ranchos. They want to prepare the sites

175

first, lay down water, drainage, and electricity, and perhaps build a little core "house" of kitchen and bathroom. Then they would let the squatters build the rest, perhaps helping them by providing cheap materials. These "do-it-yourself" houses would be much more acceptable.

The kind of city growth represented by the barrio is not a new phenomenon. Elizabethan London had its hovels outside the city gates, as did many other cities of the time. Given a moderate rate of growth, absorbing newcomers is no great problem. But in the developing world the growth rate is far from moderate. It seems impossible to build enough houses for these newcomers. Because they have virtually nothing, the expense has to be borne by the government. Shortcuts will have to be found. The "do it yourself" house is one of these, but apart from a few prototype neighborhoods outside several Latin American cities, no effective shortcut has been adopted.

Another challenge is that of absorbing the newcomers into the life and work of the city. This, also, seems to be an impossible task. Thousands of people are attempting to eke out a living as street vendors. Others have no work at all; one out of every five people in Caracas is unemployed. Beggars are a common sight. There are not enough jobs.

Even if one is lucky enough to get a job, there remains the problem of learning and adjusting to the sometimes frightening ways of the big city, which are often baffling and bewildering to a semiliterate peasant from a remote mountain village. It is not surprising that these people try to live close together, to retain some sense of the community they had at home. For them—and for millions of people throughout the world—urbanization is a very personal and very difficult process.

A street vendor in La Paz, capital of Bolivia, weighs some coffee beans for a customer. The city's name means "Peace."

Right: Plan for a *barriada*. Architect James Stirling has designed a basic structure that squatters can build onto according to their needs and resources. The central service core and the four adjacent L-shaped apartments would be provided by the government and the rest of each square filled in (around the courtyard) by the inhabitants with additional bedrooms or shops, or left vacant.

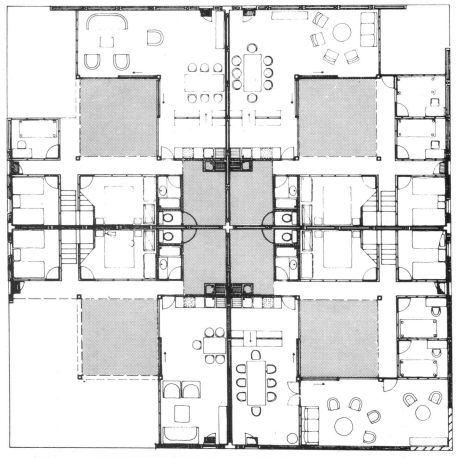

Left: Selling hope. In many countries a national lottery brings revenue to the state and offers individuals a chance to strike it rich. The sale of tickets also provides jobs for many immigrants to the city. This man combines ticket-selling with shining shoes.

177

Building for Tomorrow

8

Brasilia, the new capital of Brazil, is one of the most imposing cities ever built. Its architecture is strikingly modern (above, the main government building), but in spirit the city owes much to baroque city-planning. Peter the Great, one suspects, would have admired this city.

PEOPLE have never been entirely satisfied with the cities they have built. From time to time, someone has come up with an idea for a better city—one that would be more beautiful, more resistant to enemy attack, or more comfortable to live in. A few planners have seen their dream cities become reality. Hippodamus may have lived to see his grid plan used in building the city of Piraeus.

Titus Salt achieved his aim of creating a pleasant town for industrial workers. And in modern times, the planner Lucius Costa and his architects, Oscar Niemeyer and the Levi brothers, have seen their monumental capital city of Brasilia take shape on a vast Brazilian plain.

Most cities, however, have grown less by design than by evolution. Few medieval

179

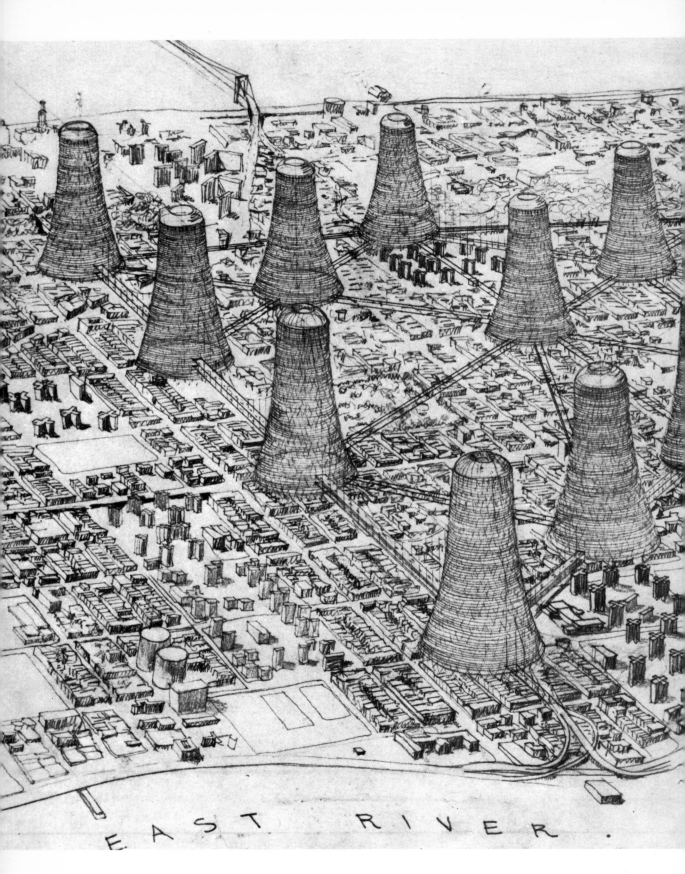

EAST RIVER.

180

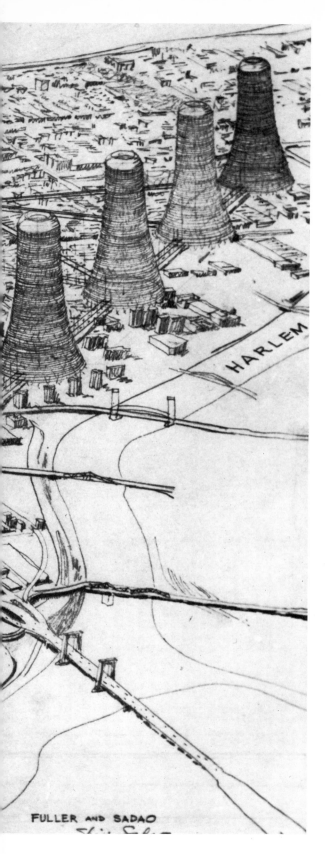

FULLER AND SADAO

This plan to transform Harlem was designed by Buckminster Fuller as an alternative to the usual kind of urban renewal, which uproots and resettles people away from their homes. Fuller's enormous towers, each housing 30,000 people, would be set on top of existing buildings and would be connected by a system of elevated highways. A central mast supports the tower, and concentric circles of shops, services, and housing are suspended between the mast and the outer network of steel cables.

cities were planned; they simply developed according to the needs of the people who lived in them. Because they were small, their unplanned nature was no serious drawback. Today, by contrast, cities have become so large that their continued random growth poses a threat not only to the surrounding countryside but also to the quality of life within the city itself. Tomorrow's cities must be planned—but planned in what way?

Some of the plans for future cities have a strong science-fiction quality. Many depend on spectacular feats of engineering, some of them still beyond our reach. But even the most far-fetched of them may in time become reality. A hundred years ago, the Empire State Building would have seemed impossible to achieve.

While some architects plan giant "wheel" cities, cave cities, and mile-high towers, most current city planning is more conservative. Some of it involves building new towns, and some has to do with improving existing cities and planning for their future growth.

One idea that has greatly influenced 20th-century town planners is that of the "garden city." The mingling of town and country goes back many centuries: we recall Petrarch's "country house in the middle of a town." But the term "garden city" dates from around the turn of the century, when an Englishman named Ebenezer Howard published a book entitled *Garden Cities of Tomorrow.*

Like many other people, Howard was appalled by the squalor of the industrial city. He was distressed by the fact that millions of people had to live in an environ-

182

Far left: The new town of Hemel Hempstead, 25 miles from London, incorporates an old village, new houses, shops, and light industry, all set in attractive countryside.
Left: In Lake Anne Village, Reston, Virginia, boys go fishing, about 100 yards from the village center. In the background are some of the town houses, which are arranged in clusters around the lakeside.
Lake Anne is the first of seven projected villages that—along with an industrial center—will eventually form Reston.

Right: An office building in Tapiola, a beautiful new town near Helsinki, Finland. The magnificent evergreens add to the appeal of this new town.

ment lacking in fresh air, sunshine, green fields, and trees. Physically, the city was a bad environment. On the other hand, he realized that socially and intellectually it was an exciting place to live. Cities attracted the best brains and produced the best ideas. The country produced only foodstuffs.

Howard proposed an environment that would combine the best of both worlds. His "garden city" was to be a complete unit. It would be economically complete in having enough land on which to grow food (only 1,000 out of a total 6,000 acres would be built on) and its own industries to provide jobs for the citizens. It would be socially complete in having shops, schools, churches, and entertainment facilities similar to those in the larger cities. The community would

183

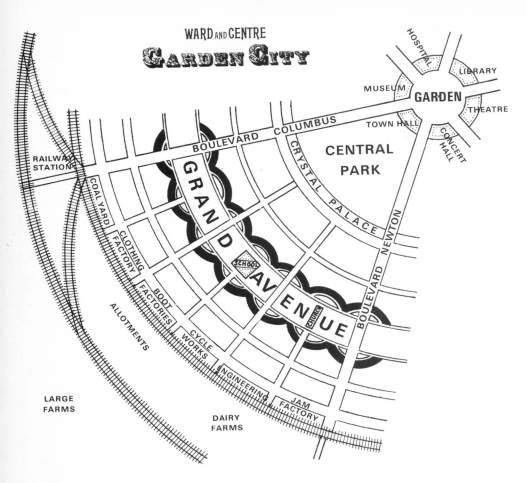

WARD AND CENTRE
GARDEN CITY

Left: Part of Ebenezer Howard's plan for a garden city. The center is a circle of cultural facilities in a large park (continued around the circle). The residential area takes up the largest part of the circle—on either side of a tree-shaded "Grand Avenue"—while industry is on the periphery near the railroad.

Left: Canberra, the capital of Australia. The green areas and abundant trees and the spread-out character of the city were inspired by Howard's garden city idea. Notice, also, the very wide avenue leading from the parliament building (foreground) to the edge of the lake. Although the city was founded as late as 1913, its plan is reminiscent of Washington, designed 100 years earlier.

be its own landlord, so that all real-estate profits would go back into the city.

Howard's diagram for a garden city—and he stressed that it was only a diagram, not a blueprint—was circular. At the center of the town would be civic and cultural buildings, a garden, and a park. Arranged in rings around this center would be shops, houses, and—at the edge of the circle—factories and the railroad station. Tree-lined roads and grand avenues and well-spaced private houses—each with its own garden—would help to create an open atmosphere within the city, and the agricultural greenbelt outside the circle would keep the city from spreading outside its limits. Howard thought that a population of about 32,000, including 2,000 farmers and agricultural workers, would be ideal for the garden city. Population growth would be dealt with not by expanding the existing city, but by creating new, separate cities.

The garden city idea found ready acceptance in England, where the countryside has always been highly prized. The first garden city was begun in 1903 around Letchworth, then a tiny village 35 miles north of London. Nearby, Welwyn Garden City was begun 20 years later. Both are prosperous towns today.

The idea of the garden city spread far beyond England. In modified forms it took root in Australia, in Scandinavia, and in the United States.

Canberra, the capital of Australia, was established in the same year that Letchworth was founded, and somewhat resembles a garden city. Its layout is very open; with an area of 961 square miles, it is larger than London or Tokyo, but it has only 120,000 inhabitants. Wide avenues radiate from a center including a government building and a beautiful lake.

The new towns inspired by the garden city idea have had varying degrees of success. Most of them provide a pleasant, healthy environment, but relatively few are the social, intellectual, and industrial "magnets" envisaged by Howard. The difficulty of attracting industry away from the big cities has resulted in many a new town being, in effect, only a suburb.

Even one of the most beautiful of the newer planned towns, Finland's Tapiola, has not realized its goal as an employer. Originally the town was intended to provide jobs (mainly in shops and light industry) for 5,650 people; but by 1965, only 2,300 people were working there, out of a resident population of 17,000. Located only six miles from Helsinki, where plenty of jobs are available, Tapiola is more dependent economically on the capital than its planners originally intended.

Even so, Tapiola is a beautiful example of town planning. It consists of a town center with shops and public buildings, an industrial zone, and three residential neighborhoods. The industrial zone is buffered from the residential areas by forest (57 per cent of the town's area is open land). Each of the three neighborhoods include houses and apartments, small shops, a kindergarten and elementary school, and a youth center.

Because the planners of Tapiola wanted to ensure that the community would include a wide range of income levels, they provided a wide range of housing. Although the single-family house is preferred by most Finns, it is

On these two pages are some of the shapes that may dominate our urban landscapes for the next few decades. Below: The ubiquitous highway "spaghetti," devourer of open countryside. looks almost beautiful, from the air. At left: A highway curves between sections of a new town in Denmark,

whose graceful circular neighborhoods suggest blossoms on a flower stalk. Right: Massive apartment houses in West Berlin are typical of modern housing throughout the world. A different approach to apartment living is Moshe Safdie's Habitat '67 (left), built near the site of Montreal's Expo '67. It consists of a number of prefabricated units of varying size, which are stacked into position in a seemingly random pattern. Elevators and pedestrian walkways link the units.

relatively expensive. To make it possible for lower income people to live in Tapiola, the planners built many row houses and apartments. They have mingled the types of housing so that each neighborhood is economically integrated and visually varied.

Similar to Tapiola in its conception is the new town of Reston, Virginia, 18 miles away from Washington D.C. The first of Reston's seven villages, Lake Anne Village, is built around an artificial lake and has, like Tapiola, a mixture of detached houses, row houses, and apartments. There is plenty of open land and wooded areas. In place of the checkerboard pattern of the typical suburban development, Lake Anne Village has clusters of houses set harmoniously in the landscape, and winding streets and pedestrian paths.

An important part of the plan for the whole of Reston is that motor and pedestrian traffic are segregated. This is not a new idea: more than 400 years ago, Leonardo da Vinci designed a town in which there would be two levels of traffic; wheeled vehicles would use the street, and pedestrians would have elevated walkways. More recently, in the 1920s, the town of Radburn, New Jersey, was planned with two separate road systems. A series of overpasses and underpasses make it possible for the two systems to overlap without actually crossing. A similar plan has been adopted at Reston. Parents with small children can send their children to school without worrying about motor traffic. Moreover, by keeping the automobile "at bay," the planners have produced an environment that clearly belongs to humans. The center of Lake Anne Village is not a busy intersection with a traffic light, but a lakefront plaza with a café and shops and (above the shops) apartments—a radical departure from the typical suburban segregation of residential and commercial areas. People can stroll around and experience the sociable atmosphere that marks so many pedestrian streets and arcades in Italian towns.

Eventually, Reston is intended to comprise seven villages and an industrial center. The goal is to provide jobs for some 30,000

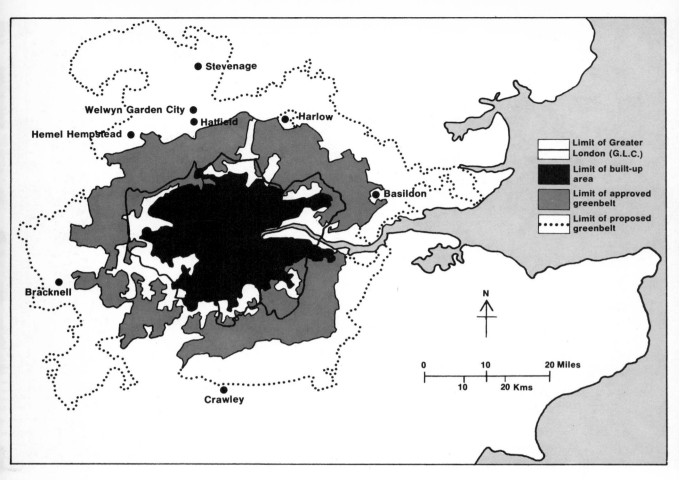

Above: This map of London and its surroundings shows the greenbelt and the location of New Towns.

Below: The Randstad embraces most of the Netherlands' major cities in two curved conurbations.

people by the year 1980. Attracting industry is difficult while the population is so low; and, conversely, attracting residents depends partly on the availability of jobs in the vicinity. Many of Lake Anne's residents now commute to Washington. Creating a truly self-sufficient community is no easy task.

Decentralization is an important trend in modern town planning. The new towns built in Britain since the last war and located beyond London's Green Belt represent one attempt to decentralize a metropolis. Their planners have drawn much of their inspiration from Howard's "garden city," particularly in seeking to create self-sufficient communities. Some of the new towns have been very successful in attracting business.

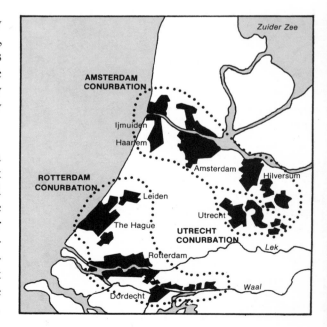

Hemel Hempstead, about half an hour from London by train, has several flourishing industries, and only a small percentage of its population commutes to London.

It is hoped that such growth by satellite (as we might call the British new towns, Reston and others) will relieve some of the pressure already experienced by the huge metropolises and prevent this pressure from becoming worse in the future.

Another pattern of decentralization is emerging in the Netherlands, which, after Monaco and Hong Kong, is the most densely populated country in the world. A number of old cities, including Amsterdam, Utrecht, Rotterdam, and The Hague, form a conurbation shaped roughly like a horseshoe. This has come to be known as the "Randstad" (Ring City). In the center of the ring is agricultural land.

As it stands, this is a very satisfactory

This photo-montage of the university area of Civilia, a proposed hill-town in Britain's Midlands, uses parts of Habitat '67, Moshe Safdie's revolutionary apartment building in Montreal, to suggest the possibility of visual excitement in a modern city.

arrangement. Each of the various cities within the Randstad has a different function: The Hague is the seat of government, Amsterdam is the commercial and cultural capital, Rotterdam the major port, and so on. This is very different from England, for example, where all these functions are concentrated in London. Each city in the Randstad is close to the others, and all are well connected by fast transport. But growth here, as elsewhere, is posing a threat. Dutch planners have adopted certain principles of growth to ensure that the agricultural land in the center is kept intact, and that the cities in the ring do not spread into each other but remain distinct.

Above: Dramatic shapes are appearing on today's urban landscape. The airport—an outpost of the city—is the modern equivalent of the Victorian railroad station (see page 118); Architect Eero Saarinen's design for Dulles International Airport (near Washington) manages to combine monumentality with an impression of flight.

Left: The provincial capital of Chandigarh, in India, was largely designed by Le Corbusier. In the foreground part of an imposing government building is mirrored in a placid lake.

The audacious architecture of Brasilia's cathedral (right) recalls, in spirit, the flying buttresses and soaring towers of the great churches of the Middle Ages. Unlike the medieval cathedral, however, this one does not dominate the entire city; it must share center stage with buildings devoted to the business of the city: government (see page 178).

Holland's Randstad developed naturally from the growth of existing cities. Other planners have proposed building *linear* cities. As early as 1882, a Spanish transport engineer, Arturo Soria y Mata, proposed building a city outside Madrid that would be a ribbon of development along a streetcar line. The rapid transit would enable citizens to reach any point in the city quickly and would also link them to Madrid. Any point in the long, narrow city would have easy access to the countryside. Although Soria y Mata's plan was never completed, the linear city idea is still alive and appears in modified forms in many contemporary city plans.

The kinds of cities we build depend very much on the amount of land available. A spread-out city with low buildings and detached houses, such as Los Angeles or Canberra, is really practical only where land is abundant. In many parts of the world, especially as population increases, we shall be forced to build cities with very high density.

Some people feel that high density is far from a bad thing. In her book *The Death and Life of Great American Cities*, Jane Jacobs points out how neighborly a city street can be. She compares the intimate life of a city street, with its neighborhood stores and people chatting on the sidewalks, with a vast empty suburb. She believes, as do many others, that it is coming together and sharing ideas that make a richer life.

One British architect, repelled by most existing urban and suburban landscapes, has proposed building hill-towns on the site of

191

"Plug-in City," designed by Peter Cook, of the London-based Archigram group of architects, would consist of a basic structure built to last for a period of 40 years, to which other units, such as housing, could be clipped on, relocated as needed, and discarded after only a few years' use. The round towers are apartments and hotels; business, industry, and entertainment centers are represented by the rectangular shapes. Rooftop tracks convey cranes to all parts of the structure to facilitate the removing and inserting of Plug-in City's components.

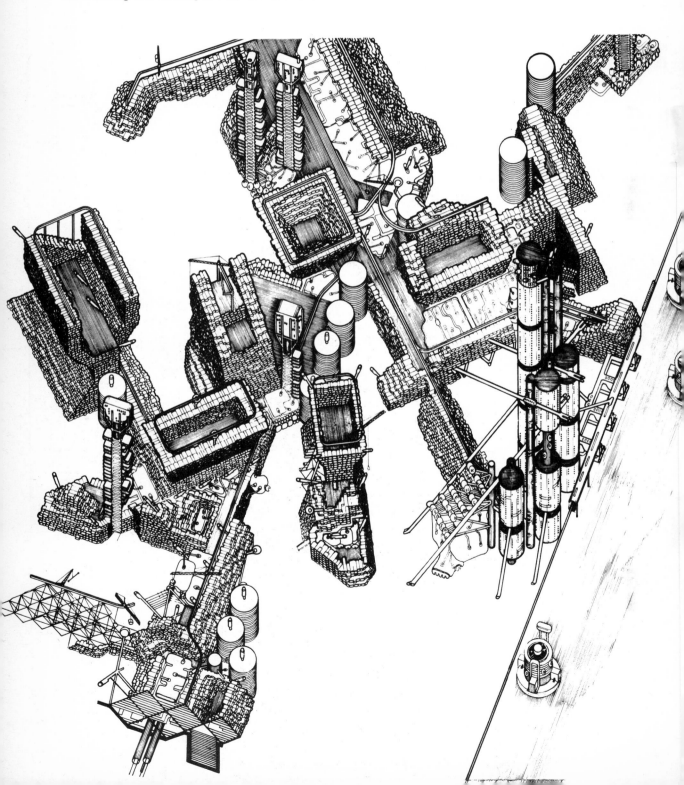

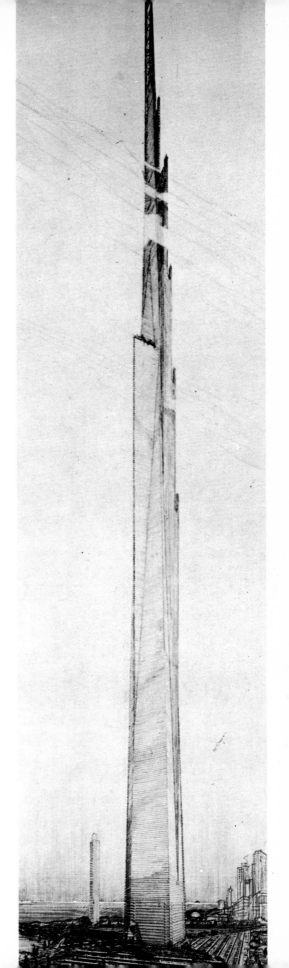

Frank Lloyd Wright's "Mile-High Sky City Illinois" (designed in 1956) is a daring plan, even by today's standards. Its tapering, sculptured form, faced with glass and steel, would be supported by a central spine reaching far into the bedrock and making the structure firm enough to withstand Chicago's ferocious winds. The central core would also accommodate the building's heating, air-conditioning, and lighting systems. Wright felt that a few such buildings would relieve the congestion in existing big cities, freeing some of the land for open countryside.

spoiltips and granite quarries in the Midlands. His model city, called "Civilia," would be a dense concentration of houses, shops, restaurants, a university, and other urban features, combined in a way that is both convenient to residents and visually exciting. The town would command a view of miles of open land, including an artificial lake and marina. Civilia would thus have a truly urban atmosphere, while offering easy access to the country.

Many city planners are trying to improve the environment within the existing, crowded cities. These are the people who have turned some town centers into pedestrian areas, where people can shop in a relaxing atmosphere away from the noise and intrusion of motor traffic. They install covered walkways and protected bus stops. They add vest-pocket parks and imaginative fountains to refresh the eye. Such "cosmetic surgery" does a great deal to improve the urban environment. Even replacing the jungles of garish commercial signs with attractive, tasteful ones would greatly improve the cities' appearance.

Meanwhile, other planners are wrestling with more basic problems. They are trying to find ways to make mass transit more efficient and to provide for increased automobile traffic without destroying the fabric of the city. They are trying to achieve a better mix of residential and commercial uses in city centers.

Ambitious redevelopment projects have been launched by a number of cities. London's Barbican Estate, now under construction, is a good example. Located near St. Paul's Cathedral, in a part of London that is almost entirely commercial, this development will eventually house 6,000 people in high-rise and low-rise apartments and town houses. The Barbican will provide shopping, cultural, and recreational facilities, linked by pedestrian walkways and beautifully landscaped with plazas, canals, and gardens. Residents will have the advantage of living close to their jobs. The drawback is that—owing to the high cost of land in the City and the consequent high property taxes—only affluent people can afford to live in the Barbican. But this sort of development, on a more modest scale, may give other citizens a more stimulating city life.

The downtown area of Montreal has been transformed by the building of Place Ville Marie. This is a vast underground complex including movie theaters, restaurants, and several hundred shops, linked by several miles of pedestrian streets and having access to a 1,000-car garage, subway and railroad lines, and above-ground office buildings. One particularly attractive feature, in view of Montreal's fierce winters and sizzling summers, is that the temperature of Place Ville Marie is stabilized at 71°F.

Climate control is a feature of many plans for tomorrow's city. Buckminster Fuller and other architects have proposed covering cities with huge plexiglass domes to shield them from the elements and noxious fumes.

People who want to avoid getting their feet wet may welcome the *omnibuilding*. This is a building that combines a number of functions under one roof. Basically, the idea is an old one: the Palace of Versailles, for example, functioned as residence, government building, and entertainment center.

More recently, the French architect and city planner Le Corbusier built his *Unité d'habitation* in Marseilles. This huge, single building houses 1,600 people and includes shops, nurseries, and recreation facilities.

American architect Lawrence Halprin has plenty of ideas for enlivening city streets and combining beauty and utility on a human scale. Far left: Children play in Halprin's Lovejoy Plaza fountain, in Portland, Oregon. A modern town clock (left) is one of the pieces of "street furniture" that he designed for Nicollet Mall, a limited-traffic street in Minneapolis. Other features of the mall: patterned brickwork around the trees, beautiful street lights (one visible), and heated bus shelters.

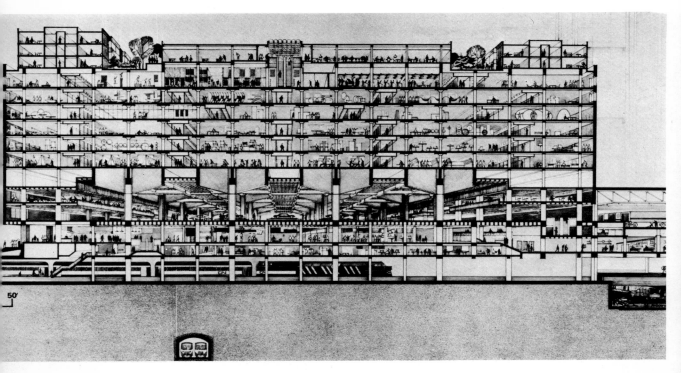

50'

The office is only an elevator ride away for some residents of Chicago's new John Hancock Center. This 100-story skyscraper is virtually a town within a town, containing not only apartments and offices, but also shops, a nursery school, an ice-skating rink, a swimming pool, a restaurant, and a hotel!

The John Hancock Center may be only a modest beginning, if some architects have their way. A Dutch architect living in England has forecast that by the year 2000 we could, if we wanted to, build towers two miles high. Each tower would hold more than 300,000 people—a medium-sized city. Each level would be a neighborhood in itself; apartments on the outside, and schools and offices near the center.

Other proposed omnibuildings are much less conventional in form than the super-skyscraper. The offshore new town for Monaco (page 200) consists of several artificial "hillsides," resembling segments of an enormous basin. The inner slopes of the "hills" would hold houses, shops, offices, cafés, and a cultural center.

Cities built out over water have obvious appeal for countries that are short of land. A Japanese architect, Kenzo Tange, has designed a solution for overcrowded Tokyo in the form of a vast network of bridges and omnibuildings to be built over Tokyo Bay. Each of the giant tent-shaped buildings would contain up to 50 stories of apartments, schools, playgrounds, and shops, as well as a

The graceful shapes in Kenzo Tange's design for
Tokyo Bay are deceptive: each building would be a
"megastructure" containing up to 50 stories on each
curved façade. The cutout areas represent public
terraces and playgrounds. Shops and other services
would be placed in the area between the curved shapes.
A system of suspended highways links the communities
to each other and to the central, man-made island
(upper right) devoted to business and industry. The
plan could be adapted to cities of 10 million or more.

Among the wilder, science-fiction-inspired designs for cities is the "walking city," designed by Ron Herron, of the Archigram group of architects. The telescoping legs of these urban monsters (note their size in relation to the Sphinx) would be capable of moving them from one region to another—possibly away from nuclear radiation. The basic idea behind this and some other cities designed by the Archigram group (see page 192) is to exploit the capabilities of machines so that they become dramatic and interesting objects in themselves.

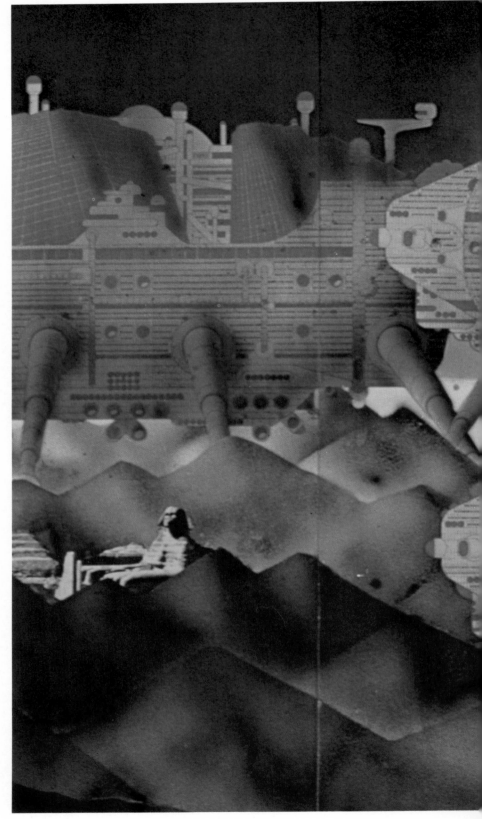

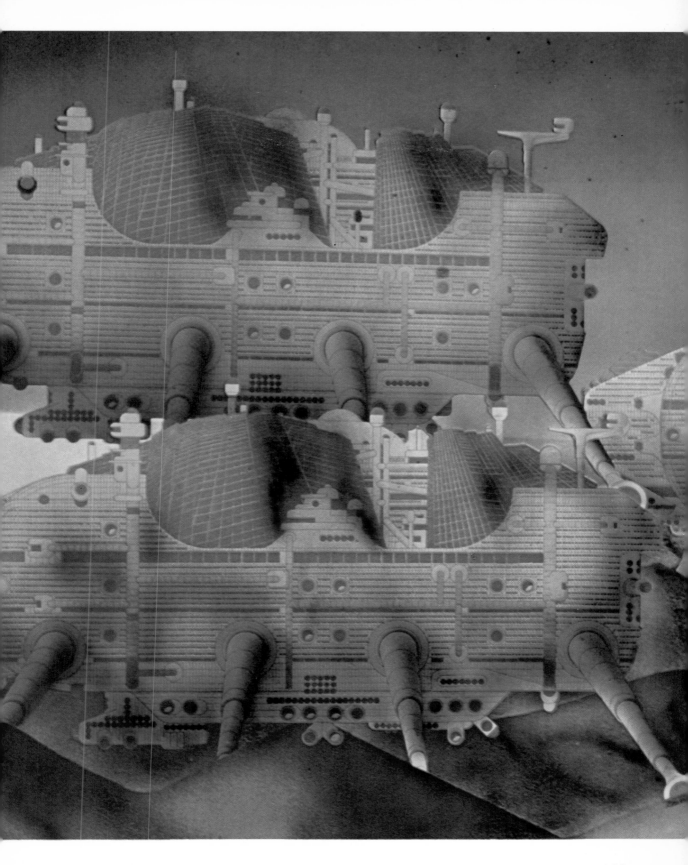

monorail station. A man-made island, running through the center of the network, would hold business and industries.

"Think big" seems to be the motto of a great many architects of tomorrow's city. This is quite understandable. The urban populations for which we must plan are getting bigger all the time. Moreover, our technology is increasingly capable of creating big solutions, and it is very tempting to exploit this capacity. If we can build two-mile-high structures, why not?

The hitch is that most people probably would not want to live in them. Many people dislike living more than 5 or 6 stories above the ground—not to mention living 50 stories above water, or 800 stories up in a two-mile-high tower. Such out-of-the-world living would demand an enormous psychological adjustment, which many—if not most—people would be incapable of making. The Greek city planner Doxiadis has warned that this kind of living "may gradually isolate man from the elements of nature, and this isolation may turn him into an inhabitant of the earth who is not interested in what happens outside his shell."

As an alternative to this "monster bee-hive," city and its opposite, the dispersed, continuous suburb city, Doxiadis proposes what he calls "Ecumenopolis." This would be a network of urban centers covering the earth, but interspersed with areas of open

Right: Now taking shape in the Arizona Desert, Paolo Soleri's "Arcosanti" will eventually house a community of 3,000 people. The 25-story structure, shown here in cross section, will occupy only 2 per cent of the 860-acre site, leaving the rest of the land in its natural state. Part of Soleri's concept of "arcology" (see page 20) is that people benefit from living in close contact with each other and with unspoiled nature—instead of in the spread-out kind of city most of us live in today. Born in Italy, Soleri went to the United States to study with Frank Lloyd Wright, and subsequently set up his own foundation to study urban design. Arcosanti is the first of his arcologies to be built. (See the following page.)

Below: An artist's drawing of a new town now being built just off the coast of the tiny principality of Monaco. It consists of an attractive grouping of concave, artificial hills, terraced and landscaped, containing housing for the town's population; shops and offices; and a cultural center. The complex will be linked by a short roadway to the mainland.

SEA DAM HOUSING TOWN CENTER HOUSING CULTURAL CENTER OLD TOWN OF MON

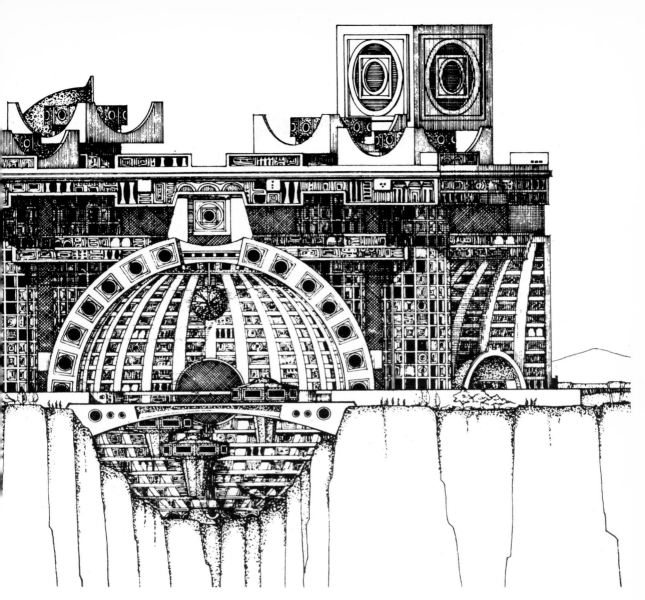

land. Some of the centers would be enormous, with populations runnings to hundreds of millions; others would be very small. But all would be composed of basic "cells," communities small enough for people to walk to their normal destinations.

We are left, basically, with two diverging tendencies in urban planning: the spread-out city, covering more and more of the land, and the high-density city with buildings and populations concentrated in relatively small areas. The future will probably offer both kinds of city. The cities we have already built will certainly continue to exist, with modifications, for many years to come.

New city building can, and should, cater for a variety of preferences. Students and young couples might prefer to live in apartments in a busy city neighborhood; families with small children might prefer a house with a garden; elderly couples might prefer to move back into an apartment near the city center. This, of course, is what is happening today, and we can reasonably assume that people's needs will remain more or less the same. But whatever new shapes appear on the urban horizon, we can expect that there will be plenty of variety, and that the idea of a city will continue to undergo new and thoughtful interpretations.

Seen through a fish-eye lens; some of the student volunteers at work constructing Arcosanti. Although still in its initial stages, the project has attracted hundreds of participants, who come for six-week workshops, to learn Soleri's principles of arcology and to apply them in building this experimental structure. When completed, Arcosanti will be a one-building university town, where people can study environmental design in a unique setting.

For Further Reading

Listed below are a few of the many good books that have been written about cities and city life.

Cities in the Motor Age, by W. Owen; The Viking Press, N.Y., 1959; Macmillan, London, 1959.

Cities of Destiny, ed. A. Toynbee; McGraw-Hill, N.Y., 1967; Thames & Hudson, London, 1967.

Cities on the Move, by A. Toynbee; Oxford University Press, New York and London, 1970.

The City in History, by L. Mumford; Secker & Warburg, London, 1961; Harcourt, Brace & World, N.Y., 1963.

The City in Newly Developing Countries, by G. Pareese; Prentice-Hall, N.Y., 1969.

The Death and Life of Great American Cities, by J. Jacobs; Random House, N.Y., 1961; Penguin Books, Harmondsworth (U.K.), 1964.

Garden Cities of Tomorrow, by E. Howard; Faber & Faber, London, 1945; Transatlantic Arts, N.Y., 1946.

The Heart of Our Cities, by Victor Gruen; Simon & Schuster, N.Y., 1964; Thames & Hudson, London, 1965.

A History of Urban America, by C. M. Glaab and A. T. Brown; Collier-Macmillan, N.Y. and London, 1967.

Images of the American City, ed. A. Strauss; Free Press of Glencoe (Crowell Collier, Macmillan), N.Y. and London, 1961.

The Italian City-Republics, by D. Waley; McGraw-Hill, N.Y., 1969; Weidenfeld & Nicholson, London, 1969.

Living in Cities, by A. Ridley; Heinemann, London, 1971; John Day, N.Y., 1972.

London, the Unique City, by S. E. Rasmussen; Macmillan, N.Y., 1937; Jonathan Cape, London, 1937.

The Making of Dutch Towns, by G. L. Burke; Cleaver-Hume Press, London, 1956; Simmons-Boardman, N.Y., 1960.

Medieval Cities, by H. Pirenne; Princeton University Press, Princeton, 1952.

Megalopolis, by J. Gottmann; The Twentieth-Century Fund, N.Y., 1961; M.I.T. Press, London, 1964.

Pompeii and Herculaneum, by M. Brion; T. Y. Crowell, N.Y., 1960; Elek Books, London, 1960.

The Rise of Urban America, by C. McL. Green; Harper & Row, N.Y., 1965; Hutchinson, London, 1966.

Town and Square: From the Agora to the Village Green, by P. Zucker; Columbia University Press, N.Y., 1959.

Towns and Buildings, by S. E. Rasmussen, M.I.T. Press, Cambridge, Mass. 1969.

Towns and Cities, by E. Jones, Oxford University Press, N.Y. and London, 1966.

The Urban Future, ed. E. Chinoy; Lieber-Atherton, N.Y., 1973.

Urban Planning in Pre-Columbian America, by J. Hardoy; Braziller, N.Y., 1968; Studio Vista, London, 1968.

Victorian Cities, by A. Briggs; Odhams Press, London, 1963; Harper & Row, N.Y., 1965.

The World Cities, by P. Hall; McGraw-Hill, N.Y., 1966; Weidenfeld & Nicholson, London, 1966.

Index

Acknowledgments

TEXT ACKNOWLEDGMENTS

Page 37 Poem adapted by Arthur F. Wright from the translation by William Hung in *Tu Fu, China's Greatest Poet*, Cambridge, Mass., 1952. Reprinted by permission.

Page 145 excerpts from "Letter from Paris," THE GUARDIAN, October 30, 1971, reprinted by permission of Nesta Roberts.

Page 168 excerpts from a broadcast from Peking by Joseph Kraft used by permission of Joseph Kraft and the British Broadcasting Corporation.

PICTURE ACKNOWLEDGMENTS

Jane Addams Memorial Collection, University of Illinois, Chicago 127(B)
Aldus Archives 36, 39(T), 184(T)
Photos © Aldus Books (Mike Busselle and Richard Hatswell) 6, 10(BR), 21, 136, 150(B), (Mark Edwards) 162(B), 163, (John Freeman) 53, (John Webb) 122
Diagrams © Aldus Books (David Cox) 26(L), (Frances De Rees) 28–29, 77(B), 152–153, 188
Peter Cook, Archigram, 1966 192
Ron Herron, Archigram, 1964 198–199
Architectural Review 189
Gerald Burke, *Towns in the Making*, Edward Arnold (Publishers) Ltd., London 69
Photo Arnott & Rogers Ltd., Montreal 196
B. Arthaud, Grenoble 45
Australian News and Information Bureau 184(B)
Peter Baistow 148, 182(L)
Bayerische Staatsbibliothek München 55(R)
Photo Roloff Beny 41(R)
Gottfried Keller Stiftung, Berne Museum 86–87
The Bettmann Archive 129(B)
Bibliothèque Nationale, Paris/Photo Françoise Foliot © Aldus Books 67(T)
Reproduced by permission of the Birmingham Museum and Art Gallery 111
Birmingham Public Libraries (Local Studies Library) 121
M. Bosc 149(R)
Bradford City Libraries 125
Reproduced by permission of the Trustees of The British Museum 35, 75
Brown Brothers 116
Camera Press 164(B)
Michael Carapagia 104–105(B)
J. Allan Cash 10(BL)
Colorific! (Les Battaglia) 106(B), (M. Bennett) 18(T), (Julian Cowan) 156, (Mary Fisher) 107(T), (T. Le Goubin) 16, (John Moss) 159(R), 174
The Cooper-Bridgeman Library 127(T)
S.S. Tommy/Cosanti Foundation 202
Daily Telegraph Color Library 147
From the collection of The Detroit Institute of Arts; Purchase, General Membership Fund 54
Elia Eliopoulo (Photocolor Labs.), Athens 177(BR)
Mary Evans Picture Library 13(T), 96–97, 100, 105(C)
Courtesy of the Fogg Art Museum, Harvard University, Bequest: Collection of Maurice Wertheim 119(R)
Fotolink 13(B), 157(B), 162(TR), 173
FPG (Sondak) 139(B), (D. Spindel) 132–133(B)
Louis H. Frohman 129(T)
Courtesy Buckminster Fuller and Shoji Sadao 180
© 1953, William Garnett 8
Musée Condé, Chantilly/Photo Giraudon 58

Susan Griggs Agency (Julian Calder) 133(T), (Victor Englebert) 170(L), 171(T), 172, 176, (John Marmaras) 110(L), (Horst Munzig) 134(B), (Reflejo) 171(B), 175(T), 178–179, 191(R), (John G. Ross) 15(BR), (Peter Sanders) 161(L), Wendy V. Watriss 15(TR), 159(BL), (Adam Woolfitt) 10(T), 19(R), 139(T)
Guildhall Library, City of London 92(B)
Lawrence Halprin & Associates 194, 195
Lewis Mumford, *The City in History*, Harcourt, Brace, and World N.Y. 1963 89(R)
Robert Harding Associates 135(R), 160(L), 161(R), 167
The John Hillelson Agency (Dr. Gerster) 12(BL), 39(B), 186(TL) (TR), (George Rodger) 24(L)
Hirmer Fotoarchiv Munich 22, 27(T)
Michael Holford Library Photo 27(C) (B)
Angelo Hornak Library 190(T)
Photo Richard Hutchings 17(R)
Irish Tourist Board 56
Kenzo Tange and Urtec, Tokyo 197
Keystone 14(T), 162(TL), 164(T)
State Museum Kröller-Müller, Otterlo 31
Leeds City Libraries 123(T)
The London Museum/British Crown Copyright, 1967 25
Magnum Photos (Ian Berry) 114(L), (Bruce Davidson) 145, (Marc Riboud) 169
Mansell/Alinari 48(C) (B), 80–81
Mansell Collection 48–49(T), 68(T), 93(T)
Bildarchiv Foto Marburg 32
Photos Eric de Maré 64(T), 118
Paulo Soleri, *Arcology: City in the Image of Man*, M.I.T. Press, 1969 21, 201
Photo Musée de Versailles 98
National Gallery, London 95, 99(R)
Courtesy of the National Ocean Survey, NOAA Department of Commerce, USA 117
Bildarchiv der Osterreichischen Nationalbibliothek, Wien 88
Photo Researchers, Inc. (V. Bucher) 140–141(T), (J. Munroe) 137
© Pictorial Maps Inc., New York, endpapers
Picturepoint, London 134(T), 154, 183(R), 187(B), 190(B)
Photo Douglas Pike & Associates 158
Josephine Powell 47(BL) (R)
Mauro Pucciarelli, Rome 14(B), 43, 46(L), 62–63, 70–71(T), 78, 82(B), 102(B)
Reproduced by permission of *Punch* 124(L)
Radio Times Hulton Picture Library 77(T), 101, 104(T), 108–109, 112, 120(L)
Rapho (de Sazo) 142(L), (Pavlovaky) 90–91
Rijksmuseum, Amsterdam 74
Padova, Palazzo della Ragione/Scala, Florence 73
Emil Schulthess 166(L)
Science Museum, London 115
Editions d'Art Albert Skira, Geneva 2
Photos Edwin Smith 40, 44, 65
Snark International 59(L)
Spectrum Color Library 18(B), 186(BL)
Preussiacher Kulturbesitz, Bildarchiv, Staatsbibliothek Berlin 57
Saul Steinberg 151(B)
Previ Low Cost Mass Housing project, Lima, Peru., Architect: James Stirling & Partners 177(T)
H. Van Haelewyn 50, 55(L)
Eleanor Van Zandt 49(R), 71(B), 102(TL), 107(R), 143, 182(R)
Victoria & Albert Museum, London. British Crown Copyright 84–85
Eduard Widmer 59(R)
The Frank Lloyd Wright Foundation 193
ZEFA (H. Adam) 61, (S. Deleu) 130, (R. Everts) 66, (Gursky-Studio) 140(B), (L. Hellmig) 103(R), (R. Hetz) 151(T), (W. H. Mueller) 70(B), (R. Pierer) 132(T), (Schneiders) 46–47(T), (K. Schulz) 42(L), (Studio Benser) 103(L)